1001
MOST USEFUL
FRENCH WORDS

Marcella Ottolenghi Buxbaum

DOVER PUBLICATIONS, INC.
Mineola, New York

Copyright

Bibliographical Note

1001 Most Useful French Words is a new work, first published by Dover Publications, Inc., in 2001. It is written as an aid for students who wish to build their French vocabularies and is patterned after *1001 Most Useful Spanish Words* by Seymour Resnick. It is he who devised its structure as a learning tool. The section "Vocabulary Tips" uses examples for minor spelling changes from L. C. Seibert & L. G. Crocker, *Skills and Techniques for Reading French,* The Johns Hopkins Press, Baltimore, 1958 (chapter 1). In the final stages of refining the book, Janet Kopito made helpful comments.

Library of Congress Cataloging-in-Publication Data

Buxbaum, Marcella Ottolenghi.
    1001 most useful French words / Marcella Ottolenghi Buxbaum.
      p. cm.
    ISBN 0-486-41944-4 (pbk.)
    1. French language—Glossaries, vocabularies, etc. I. Title: One thousand one most useful French words. II. Title: One thousand and one most useful French words. III. Title.

PC2680 .B89 2001
448.2'421—dc21

2001028621

Manufactured in the United States of America
Dover Publications, Inc., 31 East 2nd Street, Mineola, N.Y. 11501

Preface

This book contains more than 1,000 of the most useful words in the French language. They are presented in alphabetical order with simple sentences of practical value as illustrations. An English translation of each word and sample sentence follows. Below are examples:

aiguille *f.*   needle   *J'apporte toujours une aiguille avec moi quand je voyage.*   I always carry a needle with me when I travel.

aimable   pleasant   *Notre séjour a été très aimable.*   Our stay has been very pleasant.

appareil *m.*   appliance, camera   *J'ai apporté mon appareil photo, bien entendu.*   I brought my camera, of course.

The *m.* or *f.* following each noun indicates that the noun is masculine or feminine respectively. The abbreviation *pl.* stands for plural.

We suggest going through the alphabetical (or, dictionary) section quickly, checking off words that are of special interest to you. Carry this little book with you and when you see or hear a new word, look it up.

After the alphabetical list of words, ten categories of words are listed: family, days, months, seasons, numbers, colors, food, stores, professions and animals. You may wish to look through these groups of words. The vocabulary they contain is essential and is not repeated in the alphabetical section. Before going out to eat, you might check through the food category, noting items you may want to order or to avoid.

There is also a page of Vocabulary Tips showing how you can easily recognize hundreds of French/English cognates. It is advisable to spend a few minutes with this section as you begin.

Bonne chance! Good luck!

Contents

ALPHABETICAL (DICTIONARY) SECTION

à in, at, to *Il obéit à l'école mais à la maison il est difficile.* He obeys in school but at home he is difficult.

accepter to accept *Acceptez-vous la carte Visa?* Do you accept the Visa card?

accompagner to accompany, go with *Est-ce que je peux vous accompagner?* May I go with you?

accord *m.* accord, agreement *Nous sommes d'accord avec vous.* We agree with you.

acheter to buy *Nous avons acheté beaucoup de timbres.* We bought a lot of stamps.

action *f.* action *Ses actions me troublent.* His actions disturb me.

actuel present, current *Le président actuel a beaucoup d'ennemis.* The current president has many enemies.

addition *f.* check, bill (restaurant) *L'addition, s'il vous plaît.* The check, please.

adieu good-bye *Adieu et bonne chance.* Good-bye and good luck.

adresse *f.* address *Je te donnerai l'adresse d'un bon hôtel à Aix-en-Provence.* I will give you the address of a good hotel in Aix-en-Provence.

aéroport *m.* airport *L'aéroport est loin de la ville.* The airport is far from the city.

affaire *f.* matter, affair *C'est une affaire compliquée.* It's a complicated matter.

affaires *m. pl.* business dealings *Cette compagnie a beaucoup d'affaires à l'étranger.* This company has many business dealings abroad.

affectueux (euse) affectionate *Il est toujours très affectueux avec les parents.* He is always very affectionate with his relatives.

âge *m.* age *Quel âge as-tu?* How old are you?

agent (de police) *m.* police officer *Le criminel a été arrêté par deux agents de police.* The criminal was arrested by two police officers.

aider to help *Pouvez-vous nous aider?* Can you help us?

aiguille *f.*　needle　*J'apporte toujours une aiguille avec moi quand je voyage.*　I always carry a needle with me when I travel.

ailleurs; d'ailleurs　elsewhere; besides, moreover　*Il habite ailleurs, et d'ailleurs je n'ai pas envie de le voir.*　He lives elsewhere and, moreover, I don't feel like seeing him.

aimable　pleasant　*Notre séjour a été très aimable.*　Our stay has been very pleasant.

aimer　to love, like　*Il aime tellement sa petite amie qu'il la voit tous les jours.*　He loves his girlfriend so much that he sees her every day.

ainsi　thus, this way　*Si vous stationnez ainsi, je ne pourrai pas sortir de l'auto.*　If you park this way, I will not be able to get out of the car.

air *m.*　air　*Je vais ouvrir la fenêtre pour avoir de l'air.*　I'm going to open the window to get some air.

ajouter　to add　*La valise est faite et je ne peux rien ajouter.*　The suitcase is packed and I cannot add anything.

aller　to go　*Nous pouvons aller au spectacle vendredi.*　We can go to the show on Friday.

allumer　to light, to turn on　*J'ai allumé la lampe.*　I turned on the lamp.

allumette *f.*　match　*Je n'ai pas d'allumettes parce que je ne fume pas.*　I have no matches because I don't smoke.

alors　so, then, at that time　*Alors, nous étions jeunes et forts.*　At that time, we were young and strong.

améliorer　to improve　*Pour améliorer la situation, il faut travailler plus dur.*　To improve the situation, we must work harder.

amende *f.*　fine　*Si tu laisses aller ton chien libre dans le parc, tu recevras une amende.*　If you allow your dog to go free in the park, you will receive a fine.

ami(e) *m./f.*　friend　*Je suis venu vous faire visite avec des amis.*　I came to visit you with some friends.

amitié *f.*　friendship　*Notre amitié m'est très importante.*　Our friendship is very important to me.

amitiés, faire ses __ à　to give one's regards to　*Fais mes amitiés à ta famille.*　I give my regards to your family.

amour *m.*　love　*Sans ton amour ma vie serait très triste.*　Without your love, my life would be very sad.

amoureux (euse)　in love　*Il est amoureux de sa voisine et désire l'épouser.*　He is in love with his neighbor and wants to marry her.

amuser, s'　to have a good time, to enjoy oneself　*Nous nous sommes amusés au théâtre hier soir.*　We had a good time at the theater last night.

an *m.* year *Je suis allé en France il y a deux ans.* I went to France two years ago.

anglais *m.* English *On parle anglais partout dans le monde maintenant.* English is spoken everywhere in the world now.

Angleterre *f.* England *L'Angleterre et la France sont séparées par la Manche.* England and France are separated by the English Channel.

anniversaire *m.* birthday *Je lui donne un bracelet pour son anniversaire.* I am giving her a bracelet for her birthday.

annonce *f.* advertisement *J'ai lu dans les petites annonces du journal qu'il y a un appartement à louer près d'ici.* I read in the newspaper advertisements that there is an apartment for rent near here.

appareil *m.* appliance, camera *J'ai apporté mon appareil photo, bien entendu.* I brought my camera, of course.

appartenir to belong *A qui appartient ce parapluie?* To whom does this umbrella belong?

appeler to call; **s'appeler** to be named *Il s'appelle Lawrence mais tout le monde l'appelle Larry.* He is named Lawrence but everyone calls him Larry.

apporter to bring *N'apportez pas trop de vêtements quand vous voyagez.* Don't bring too much clothing when you travel.

apprendre to learn *On apprend beaucoup en voyageant.* We learn a lot while traveling.

approcher, s' __ de to draw near to *Approchez-vous de l'ordinateur et lisez cet email.* Come closer to the computer and read this email.

après after *Nous pouvons nous reposer après le déjeuner.* We can rest after lunch.

après-midi *m./f.* afternoon *Le train part à trois heures de l'après-midi.* The train leaves at 3:00 P.M.

arbre *m.* tree *Il y a beaucoup d'arbres fruitiers dans ce jardin.* There are many fruit trees in this garden.

argent *m.* silver, money *Il faut que j'aille à la banque prendre encore d'argent.* I must go to the bank to get more money.

argent comptant *m.* cash *Il faut payer en argent comptant.* We must pay in cash.

armée *f.* army *L'armée protège la frontière entre la France et l'Espagne.* The army is protecting the border between France and Spain.

armoire *f.* wardrobe, closet *Ma chambre a une grande armoire.* My room has a large closet.

arranger to arrange, to organize, to settle *Avez-vous arrangé les choses pour notre départ?* Have you arranged things for our departure?

arrêt *m.*   stop   *L'arrêt d'autobus est au coin de cette rue.*   The bus stop is at the corner of this street.

arrêter, s'   to stop   *Arrêtez-vous au kiosque pour acheter le journal.* Stop at the newsstand to buy the paper.

arrière (en)   behind   *Il est tombé en arrière dans son travail.*   He fell behind in his work.

arrivée *f.*   arrival   *Nous attendons avec impatience l'arrivée de notre chère amie.*   We are awaiting impatiently the arrival of our dear friend.

arriver   to arrive; to happen, to occur   *La TGV (train à grande vitesse) de Paris arrive à dix heures.*   The express train from Paris arrives at ten o'clock.   *Mon Dieu, qu'est-ce qui est arrivé?*   Good Lord, what happened?

art *m.*   art   *Une des plus belles collections d'art du monde est au Louvre.*   One of the most beautiful art collections in the world is at the Louvre.

article *m.*   article   *Cet article est très intéressant. Lisez-le.*   This article is very interesting. Read it.

ascenseur *m.*   elevator   *Heureusement, il y a un ascenseur dans notre hôtel.*   Fortunately, there is an elevator in our hotel.

asseoir, s'   to sit down   *Asseyons-nous ici.*   Let's sit down here.

assez de   enough, sufficient   *Nous avons assez d'argent pour payer l'hôtel.*   We have enough money to pay for the hotel.

assister à   to attend   *J'aimerais assister à cette conférence.*   I would like to attend that lecture.

assurance *f.*   insurance   *Avez-vous l'assurance contre l'incendie?*   Do you have fire insurance?

assurer   to insure   *J'aimerais assurer ce paquet.*   I would like to insure this package.

attention *f.*   attention, care   *Attention! Ne te brûle pas.*   Careful! Don't burn yourself.

aucun(e)   none   *Aucune des chambres n'est prête.*   None of the rooms is ready.

aujourd'hui *m./f.*   today   *C'est aujourd'hui dimanche.*   Today is Sunday.

aussi   also, too   *Achetez du pain, du jambon, et une bouteille de vin aussi.*   Buy some bread, some ham, and a bottle of wine too.

autobus *m.*   bus   *L'arrêt d'autobus est au coin de cette rue.*   The bus stop is at the corner of this street.

autorité *f.*   authority   *Cet agent de police a l'autorité de nous faire une amende.*   This police officer has the authority to make us pay a fine.

autoroute *f.*   highway   *En France on a de très bonnes autoroutes.*   In France there are very good highways.

autre   other, another   *Montrez-moi une autre cravate s'il vous plaît.* Show me another tie, please.

autres, les   the rest, the others   *Les autres viendront bientôt.* The rest of them will come soon.

avant de   before   *Avant d'aller à Cannes, nous avons acheté des maillots de bain.* Before going to Cannes we bought bathing suits.

avantage *m.*   advantage   *Elle a l'avantage d'être bilingue.* She has the advantage of being bilingual.

avec   with   *J'aimerais faire cette excursion avec vous.* I would like to take that trip with you.

avenue *f.*   avenue   *L'Avenue des Champs Elysées est très belle et très élégante.* The Avenue of the Champs Elysées is very beautiful and very elegant.

avertir   to warn, notify   *Voulez-vous bien m'avertir quand je dois descendre?* Will you please let me know when I have to get off?

avertissement *m.*   warning, notification   *J'ai reçu l'avertissement que nous devons déménager dans un mois.* I received notification that we must move out in one month.

aveugle   blind   *Le chien loup aide l'homme aveugle à traverser la rue.* The seeing-eye dog helps the blind man to cross the street.

avion *m.*   airplane   *A quelle heure arrive l'avion de Nice?* At what time does the plane from Nice arrive?

avoir   to have   *J'ai beaucoup de travail à faire.* I have a lot of work to do.

bagage(s) *m.*   luggage   *On a perdu mes bagages ou bien ils les ont mis dans un autre avion.* My luggage has been lost or else they have put it on another airplane.

bague *f.*   ring   *J'ai acheté cette bague de corail au Marché aux puces.* I bought this coral ring at the Flea Market.

baiser *m.*   kiss   *Je t'envoie mille baisers.* I send you a thousand kisses.

bal *m.*   dance   *Il y a un bal à la Maison française vendredi prochain.* There is a dance at the French House next Friday.

balle *f.*   ball   *Jetez-moi la balle.* Throw me the ball.

bande *f.*   tape, (audio)cassette   *J'ai acheté plusieurs bandes de chants folkloriques.* I bought several audiotapes of folk songs.

banque *f.*   bank   *Il faut aller à la banque pour changer de l'argent.* We must go to the bank to exchange some money.

barbe *f.*   beard   *Mon fils a la barbe noire.* My son has a black beard.

bas   low   *Le plafond est très bas dans cette salle.* The ceiling is very low in this room.

bas (en)   downstairs, below   *Je t'attends en bas.* I'll wait for you downstairs.

bas *m.* stocking *Je vais mettre les bas parce qu'il fait froid.* I am going to put on stockings because it is cold.

bateau *m.* boat, ship *Il faut traverser le lac en bateau.* We must go across the lake by boat.

bâtiment *m.* building *Ce bâtiment est ancien.* This building is ancient.

beau, belle handsome, beautiful *Paris est une des plus belles villes du monde.* Paris is one of the most beautiful cities in the world.

beaucoup much, a lot *Je m'amuse beaucoup à la plage.* I enjoy myself very much at the beach.

besoin *m.* need *J'ai besoin d'y aller.* I need to go there.

bibliothèque *f.* library *Elle étudie à la bibliothèque après l'école.* She studies in the library after school.

bien well *Il joue bien du piano.* He plays the piano well.

bien que although *Bien qu'elle soit en retard, je suis sûr qu'elle arrivera.* Although she is late, I am sure she will arrive.

bientôt soon *A bientôt!* See you soon!

bienvenu(e) welcome *Soyez le bienvenu en France!* Welcome to France!

bijou *m.* jewel *Il désire acheter un bijou de valeur pour sa fille.* He wishes to buy a valuable jewel for his daughter.

billet *m.* note; ticket; bill (banknote) *Ecrivez-lui un billet pour la remercier.* Write her a note to thank her.

blouse *f.* blouse *Cette blouse te va bien.* That blouse fits you well.

boire to drink *Si vous devez conduire, il ne faut pas boire.* If you have to drive, you must not drink.

bois *m.* wood, woods *J'ai une jolie boîte de bois pour garder ma bijouterie.* I have a pretty wooden box to keep my jewelry in. *Le Bois de Boulogne a de très jolis jardins.* The Boulogne woods has many pretty gardens.

boisson *f.* drink, beverage *Prenons quelque chose à boire.* Let's have something to drink.

bon, bonne good *Bon voyage!* Have a good trip!

bon marché cheap, inexpensive *Ce bracelet est très bon marché.* This bracelet is very inexpensive.

bouche *f.* mouth *Il n'a pas ouvert la bouche tout le soir.* He didn't open his mouth all evening.

boucle (d'oreilles) *f.* earring *Dans cette bijouterie il y a de jolies boucles d'oreilles.* In this jewelry store there are some pretty earrings.

bouteille *f.* bottle *Portez la bouteille sans la rompre.* Carry the bottle without breaking it.

bracelet *m.* bracelet *Un bracelet est un bon cadeau pour ma soeur.* A bracelet is a good gift for my sister.

bras *m.* arm *Il s'est cassé le bras.* He broke his arm.

brièvement briefly *Elle m'a dit brièvement ce qui s'est passé.* She told me briefly what happened.

brosse *f.* brush *On peut acheter une brosse à dents dans la pharmacie.* One can buy a toothbrush at the pharmacy.

brouillard *m.* fog *Il y a souvent du brouillard le matin.* There is often fog in the morning.

bruit *m.* noise, rumor *Il y a trop de bruit dans cette discothèque.* There is too much noise in this disco.

brûler to burn *Tu as brûlé les pommes frites.* You burned the French fries.

brune *f.* brunette *Il a connu une jolie brune à la soirée.* He met a pretty brunette at the evening party.

budget *m.* budget *Le budget ne permet pas cette dépense.* The budget does not allow for this expenditure.

bureau *m.* office *Venez me voir dans mon bureau.* Come to see me in my office.

but *m.* goal, purpose *Le but de ma visite est de te persuader à m'accompagner à faire une excursion.* The purpose of my visit is to persuade you to take a trip with me.

cacher, se to hide (oneself) *La petite fille s'est cachée dans l'armoire.* The little girl hid in the closet.

cadeau *m.* gift *On peut acheter les cadeaux dans les grands magasins.* We can buy the gifts in the department stores.

cafétéria *f.* cafeteria *Il y a une cafétéria à l'université.* There is a cafeteria in the university.

cahier *m.* notebook *J'ai apporté un petit cahier où je vais écrire mes observations.* I brought a small notebook where I am going to write my observations.

caisse *f.* box, cash register *Payez à la caisse.* Pay at the cash register.

caissier (ière) cashier *Le caissier prendra le billet de cent francs.* The cashier will take the one-hundred-franc bill.

calculatrice *f.* calculator *Nous utilisons une calculatrice pour faire nos comptes.* We use a calculator to do our accounts.

calme calm, still, quiet *Je désire dîner dans un restaurant calme.* I want to eat dinner in a quiet restaurant.

caméscope *m.* camcorder *Nous apportons notre caméscope pour faire des films pendant le voyage.* We are bringing our camcorder to take movies during the trip.

camion *m.* truck *Quand je conduis, j'évite toujours les camions.* When I drive, I always avoid trucks.

campagne *f.* country, countryside *Nous allons à la campagne le week-end.* We go to the country on weekends.

canapé *m.*   couch   *Ce canapé est très confortable.*   This couch is very comfortable.

capital *m.*   capital (money)   *Il a envesti son capital dans le commerce de l'acier.*   He invested his capital in the steel trade.

capitale *f.*   capital (city)   *Paris est la capitale de la France.*   Paris is the capital of France.

carte *f.*   card; map; menu   *J'ai reçu une carte postale de mon ami à Lyon.*   I received a postcard from my friend in Lyon.   *Cette carte routière est très utile.*   This road map is very useful.

cas *m.*   case, matter   *C'est un cas curieux.*   It's a strange matter.

cassé(e)   broken   *La table est cassée; il faut la réparer.*   The table is broken; it must be repaired.

cathédrale *f.*   cathedral   *La cathédrale de Notre Dame à Paris date du moyen-age.*   Notre Dame Cathedral in Paris dates from the Middle Ages.

ce, cet *m.* **(cette** *f.*; **ces** *pl.*)   this, that, these, those   *Je me souviens de ces beaux jours.*   I remember those beautiful days.

ceinture *f.*   belt   *Il faut attacher les ceintures de sécurité en avion.*   You must fasten your safety belts in a plane.

célèbre   famous   *Victor Hugo est un très célèbre auteur français.*   Victor Hugo is a very famous French writer.

célibataire *m./f.*   bachelor; single, unmarried   *S'il était célibataire, je l'épouserais.*   If he were a bachelor, I would marry him.

centre-ville *m.*   business district   *Allons au centre-ville pour faire nos achats.*   Let's go downtown to do our shopping.

certain   sure, certain   *Il est certain qu'elle partira demain.*   It is sure that she will leave tomorrow.

chacun(e)   each one   *Chacun fait à sa guise.*   Each one does as he likes.

chaise *f.*   chair   *Cette chaise va bien pour l'ordinateur.*   This chair is suitable for the computer.

chaleur *f.*   heat   *On ferme les magasins l'après-midi à cause de la chaleur.*   Stores are closed in the afternoon because of the heat.

chambre *f.*   bedroom   *Toutes les chambres ont une salle de bains et un téléviseur.*   All the bedrooms have a bathroom and a television set.

champ *m.*   field   *Ce champ est plein de blé.*   This field is full of wheat.

chance *f.*   luck   *J'ai eu la bonne chance de le trouver chez lui.*   I had the good luck to find him at home.

change *m.*   exchange   *Allons au change pour échanger des dollars en francs.*   Let's go to the exchange to exchange some dollars for francs.

changer   to change   *Il a beaucoup changé depuis sa visite à Nice.*   He has changed a lot since his visit to Nice.

chanson *f.* song *C'est une chanson d'amour.* It is a love song.

chanter to sing *Mes enfants aiment chanter en voiture.* My children like to sing in the car.

chapeau *m.* hat *Il a acheté un chapeau de paille pour se réparer du soleil.* He bought a straw hat to protect himself from the sun.

château *m.* castle *A Avignon on peut visiter le château du pape.* In Avignon one can visit the Pope's castle.

chaud(e) hot *J'aimerais du thé chaud, s'il vous plaît.* I would like some hot tea, please.

chauffeur *m.* driver *Le chauffeur criait parce que la voiture devant lui ne bougeait pas.* The driver was shouting because the car in front of him wasn't moving.

chaussette *f.* sock *Apportez des chaussettes de laine pour la montagne.* Bring wool socks for the mountains.

chemin *m.* path, road *Ce chemin porte à la rivière.* This road leads to the river.

chemin (de fer) *m.* railroad *J'irai d'Italie en France par chemin de fer.* I shall go from Italy to France by railroad.

chemise *f.* shirt *L'été, je porte les chemises de coton.* In the summer, I wear cotton shirts.

chèque *m.* check *Je peux vous payer avec un chèque personnel?* Can I pay you with a personal check?

cher expensive, dear *Les vêtements sont plus chers ici qu'aux Etats-Unis.* Clothes are more expensive here than in the United States.

chercher to look for *Cherchez la clé de cette malle, Anne.* Look for the key to this trunk, Ann.

cheveu *m.* hair *Je dois me faire couper les cheveux.* I must get my hair cut.

choisir to choose, select *Nous avons choisi un hôtel près du métro.* We chose a hotel near the subway.

chose *f.* thing *Cette estampe de Daumier est la plus belle chose que j'ai achetée comme souvenir de Paris.* This Daumier print is the most beautiful thing that I have bought as a souvenir of Paris.

ciel *m.* sky *Le ciel est couvert aujourd'hui.* The sky is covered with clouds today.

cinéma *m.* movies, movie theater *Hier soir, nous avons vu un film émouvant au cinéma.* Last night, we saw a touching film at the movies.

ciseaux *m. pl.* scissors *C'est une bonne idée d'apporter des ciseaux à ongles.* It's a good idea to bring nail scissors.

clair light (color), clear *Je préfère un bleu plus clair pour cette chambre.* I prefer a lighter blue for that bedroom.

classe *f.* class *J'ai deux classes demain matin.* I have two classes tomorrow morning.

clé/clef *f.* key *Je te donne la clé de la maison mais ne la perd pas.* I am giving you the key to the house but don't lose it.

client(e) client, customer *Nous avons beaucoup de clients pendant l'été.* We have many customers in the summer.

climat *m.* climate *Le climat dans le Midi est idéal.* The climate in the south of France is ideal.

cloche *f.* bell *On entend la cloche de l'église d'ici.* We hear the church bell from here.

cœur *m.* heart *Quand j'ai su qu'elle était guérie, mon cœur c'est rempli de gratitude.* When I heard that she was cured, my heart was full of gratitude.

coin *m.* corner *L'arrêt d'autobus est au coin de cette rue.* The bus stop is at the corner of this street.

coller to paste *J'ai collé l'affiche "Défense de fumer" sur ma porte.* I pasted the sign "No smoking" on my door.

collier *m.* necklace *Le collier de diamants était faux.* It was a fake diamond necklace.

collision *f.* **(entrer en)** to collide, to crash *Les deux voitures sont entrées en collision à l'intersection.* The two cars collided at the intersection.

combien? how much? *Combien coûte ce livre?* How much does this book cost?

comme like, as *Le nouveau film de Veber, "Le Dîner des cons," comme son film célèbre "La Cage aux folles," est très amusant.* Veber's new movie, *Le Dîner des cons* (Dinner of Fools), like his famous film *La Cage aux folles* (The Birdcage), is very amusing.

commencer to begin *Elle commence déjà à lire et à écrire.* She is already beginning to read and write.

commode *f.* chest of drawers *Il y a deux commodes dans cette chambre.* There are two chests of drawers in this bedroom.

compagnie *f.* company *La compagnie Coty vend des parfums.* The Coty company sells perfumes.

complet *m.* suit, outfit *Il me semble qu'un complet suffit pour ce voyage.* It seems to me that one suit is sufficient for this trip.

comprendre to understand *Comprenez-vous le guide?* Do you understand the guide?

compter to count *Comptez l'argent qui vous reste pour voir s'il faut aller à la banque.* Count how much money you have left to see if we must go to the bank.

conduire to drive, to lead *Il va vous conduire à l'aéroport.* He is going to drive you to the airport.

conférence *f.* lecture, conference *La conférence sur les artistes impressionistes était intéressante.* The lecture on the Impressionist painters was interesting.

confortable comfortable *Ce canapé n'est pas confortable.* This couch is not comfortable.

confus confused, embarrassed *Je suis confus. Où dois-je aller?* I am confused. Where should I go?

connaître to know; to meet *Je connais les parents de mon étudiant.* I know my student's parents.

conseiller to advise *Le médecin m'a conseillé de me reposer.* The doctor advised me to rest.

consulat *m.* consulate *Si tu as perdu ton passeport, va au consulat pour en obtenir un autre.* If you have lost your passport, go to the consulate to get another one.

conte *m.* story, tale *Les enfants aiment les contes de fées.* Children like fairy tales.

content pleased, glad *Je suis très content de ton progrès.* I am very pleased with your progress.

continuer to continue, go on *Continuez à marcher tout droit et vous verrez l'arrêt d'autobus au coin de la rue.* Continue to walk straight ahead and you will see the bus stop at the corner of the street.

contraire contrary *Au contraire, il n'a jamais dit qu'il ne nous aiderait pas.* On the contrary, he never said that he would not help us.

contre against *La plupart des Français sont contre la peine capitale.* Most French people are against capital punishment.

copain, copine pal, good friend *J'aime causer avec mes copains après l'école.* I like to chat with my pals after school.

corbeille *f.* basket *J'ai jeté les papiers dans la corbeille.* I threw the papers in the basket.

corps *m.* body *On va apprendre les parties du corps en français.* We will learn the parts of the body in French.

correct correct *Cette phrase n'est pas correcte. Il y a une faute d'orthographe.* This sentence is not correct. There is a spelling mistake.

corriger to correct *Voici le brouillon du manuscrit mais il faut encore corriger les fautes.* Here is the rough draft of the manuscript but the errors still have to be corrected.

côte *f.* coast *La Côte d'Azur a de très belles plages.* The coast of the French Riviera has very beautiful beaches.

côté *m.* side *Son bureau est de l'autre côté de la rue.* His office is on the other side of the street.

coton *m.* cotton *J'aime les vêtements de coton l'été.* I like cotton clothing in the summer.

cou *m.* neck *J'ai mal au cou.* My neck hurts.

coucher, se to go to bed *Nous devons nous coucher tôt ce soir.* We must go to bed early tonight.

coudre   to sew   *Je n'aime pas coudre mais il faudra que je raccourcisse ce pantalon.*   I don't like to sew but I shall have to shorten these trousers.

coup *m.*   blow   *Le voleur a reçu un coup de bâton aux jambes et il a été arrêté.*   The thief received a blow to the legs from a billy club and he was arrested.

coupe *f.*   goblet, (sports prize) cup   *La France a gagné la Coupe du monde au football en 1990.*   France won the World Cup in soccer in 1998.

couper   to cut   *Ce couteau ne coupe pas bien.*   This knife doesn't cut well.

courir   to run   *Il faudra courir pour attraper le train.*   We will have to run to catch the train.

courrier *m.*   mail, post   *Je n'ai pas encore reçu mon courrier.*   I haven't received my mail yet.

cours *m.*   course, class   *Mon cours de littérature m'intéresse beaucoup.*   My literature course interests me a lot.

court   short   *Viens par ici. C'est plus court.*   Come this way. It's shorter.

couteau *m.*   knife   *Je n'ai pas de couteau.*   I don't have a knife.

coûter   to cost   *Combien coûte ce parapluie?*   How much does this umbrella cost?

coutume *f.*   custom   *Les coutumes changent de région en région.*   The customs vary from region to region.

couverture *f.*   blanket   *J'aurai besoin d'une couverture de laine parce qu'il fait froid la nuit.*   I shall need a wool blanket because it is cold at night.

couvrir   to cover   *Il faut couvrir les meubles avant de peindre les murs.*   We must cover the furniture before painting the walls.

cravate *f.*   tie   *J'ai acheté une belle cravate de soie pour mon oncle.*   I bought a beautiful silk tie for my uncle.

crayon *m.*   pencil   *Ne vous servez pas d'un crayon pour écrire l'examen.*   Don't use a pencil to write the exam.

cri *m.*   shout   *Un cri dans la nuit m'a fait peur.*   A shout in the night frightened me.

crier   to shout   *L'enfant a crié, "Attention, un serpent!"*   The child shouted, "Watch out, a snake!"

crime *m.*   crime   *Il a passé trois ans en prison pour son crime.*   He spent three years in jail for his crime.

croire   to believe, think   *Je crois qu'il faut réfléchir avant de faire cette décision.*   I think we must think it over before making this decision.

croix *f.*   cross   *Il n'y avait qu'une simple croix blanche pour marquer la tombe du soldat.*   There was only a simple white cross to mark the soldier's tomb.

cru raw *Si on peut les digérer, les légumes crus font bien à la santé.* If you can digest them, raw vegetables are good for your health.

cuiller/cuillère *f.* spoon *Garçon, j'ai besoin d'une cuillère.* Waiter, I need a spoon.

cuir *m.* leather *Je cherche une serviette de cuir.* I am looking for a leather briefcase.

cuisine *f.* kitchen, cooking *Cette cuisine est très moderne et jolie.* This kitchen is very modern and pretty.

cuisine, faire la to do the cooking *Qui fait la cuisine chez vous?* Who does the cooking at your house?

cuisinier (ière) cook *Le cuisinier prépare des repas délicieux.* The cook prepares delicious meals.

cuisinière *f.* stove *Cette cuisinière est facile à utiliser.* This stove is easy to use.

curé *m.* priest *Le curé les a mariés dimanche passé.* The priest married them last Sunday.

dame *f.* lady *Messieurs, dames, asseyez-vous, s'il vous plaît.* Ladies and gentlemen, please sit down.

danger *m.* danger *Evitez le danger de glisser sur la glace.* Avoid the danger of slipping on the ice.

dangereux (euse) dangerous *Cette plage est dangereuse la nuit.* This beach is dangerous at night.

danser to dance *On a dansé jusqu'à minuit.* We danced until midnight.

date *f.* date *Quelle est la date aujourd'hui?* What is today's date?

de of, from *Combien de kilomètres y a-t-il d'ici à la gare?* How many kilometers is it from here to the railroad station?

décider to decide *Eh bien, avez-vous décidé?* Well, have you decided?

découvrir to discover *J'ai découvert un restaurant près d'ici qui sert un bon repas.* I have discovered a restaurant near here which serves a good meal.

dedans inside *A l'extérieur cet immeuble n'est pas remarquable, mais si vous regardez dedans il y a une cour avec un très beau jardin.* On the outside this building is not remarkable, but if you look inside there is a courtyard with a very beautiful garden.

défendre to defend, to forbid *Il est défendu de fumer.* It is forbidden to smoke.

dehors outside *Il fait froid dehors aujourd'hui.* It is cold outside today.

déjà already *Je savais déjà qu'elle s'était fiancée.* I already knew that she had become engaged.

déjeuner *m.* lunch *En France on prend le déjeuner vers deux heures.* In France lunch is eaten at around two.

déjeuner, petit *m.*   breakfast   *A cet hôtel on sert le petit déjeuner de 7h à 10h.*   In this hotel breakfast is served from 7:00 A.M. to 10:00 A.M.

déjeuner   to eat lunch   *Elle déjeune près du bureau où elle travaille.* She eats lunch near the office where she works.

demain   tomorrow   *Je vous téléphonerai demain matin.*   I'll call you tomorrow morning.

demander   to ask (for)   *J'ai demandé au garçon où se trouve la poste.*   I asked the waiter where the post office is located.

demi   half   *Je me suis couché à minuit et demi.*   I went to bed at half past midnight.

dent *f.*   tooth   *J'ai un mal de dents terrible.*   I have a terrible toothache.

départ *m.*   leaving, departure   *Le départ de mon avion a eu un délai de deux heures.*   The departure of my plane had a two-hour delay.

dépêcher, se   to hurry   *Dépêchez-vous! Il faut partir.*   Hurry up! We have to leave.

dépendre de   to depend on   *Je ne sais pas. Ça dépend du prix.*   I don't know. It depends on the price.

dépenser   to spend   *Je dois dépenser l'argent qui me reste seulement pour des choses essentielles.*   I must spend the money remaining to me only for essential things.

depuis   since   *Il est parti pour Paris et je ne l'ai pas vu depuis.*   He left for Paris and I haven't seen him since.

déranger   to disturb, to bother   *Ne me dérangez pas!*   Do not disturb me!

dernier (ière)   last   *C'est la dernière fois que je l'ai vu.*   That's the last time I saw him.

derrière   behind, in back of   *Derrière le musée il y a un joli parc.* Behind the museum, there is a pretty park.

des   some   *J'ai apporté des sandales.*   I brought some sandals.

descendre   to go down, get off   *Nous devons descendre à l'arrêt prochain.*   We must get off at the next stop.

désirer   to want, wish, desire   *Nous désirons aller à la plage.*   We want to go to the beach.

dessein *m.*   drawing   *Dans le Musée Picasso à Paris, il y a des peintures et des desseins formidables!*   In the Picasso Museum in Paris, there are marvelous paintings and drawings!

destination *f.*   destination   *Prenez le train avec la destination Gare Montparnasse.*   Take the train that is going to the Montparnasse railroad station.

devant   in front of   *J'espère que personne ne s'assied devant nous.*   I hope no one sits down in front of us.

développer   to develop, unfold   *Le gouvernement essaie de développer* *l'énergie solaire.* The government is trying to develop solar energy. *J'ai donné la pellicule du voyage à développer.* I gave the film of the trip to be developed.

devoir to have to, must, to owe *Les étudiants doivent étudier davantage.* The students must study more.

Dieu *m.* God *Dieu merci, il pleut enfin.* Thank God, it is finally raining.

difficile difficult, hard *Il est difficile de laisser sa patrie.* It is difficult to leave one's homeland.

dire to say, tell *Tout ce qu'il dit est vrai.* Everything he says is true.

dire au revoir to say good-bye *Il faut dire au revoir à notre guide.* We must say good-bye to our guide.

distance *f.* distance *Quelle est la distance d'ici au Louvre?* What is the distance from here to the Louvre?

doigt *m.* finger *Il s'est coupé le doigt avec le couteau.* He cut his finger with the knife.

dollar *m.* dollar *L'Euro vaut à peu près un dollar aujourd'hui.* The Euro is worth approximately one dollar today.

domestique *m./f.* domestic, servant *Cette famille riche a beaucoup de domestiques.* That rich family has many servants.

dommage *m.* harm, shame, pity *Quel dommage qu'il soit tombé!* What a pity that he fell!

donner to give *Je donne toujours quelque chose aux charités.* I always give something to charities.

dorénavant from now on *Dorénavant, n'oubliez pas la clé.* From now on, don't forget the key.

dormir to sleep *Malgré la pluie, j'ai bien dormi la nuit dernière.* Despite the rain I slept well last night.

douane *f.* customs *Il faut passer par la douane à votre arrivée.* It is necessary to go through customs at your arrival.

douche *f.* shower *Je fais une douche tous les matins.* I take a shower every morning.

douleur *f.* pain, ache *J'ai une douleur au cou.* I have a pain in my neck.

douter (de) to doubt *Il dit que la chambre sera prête dans vingt minutes mais j'en doute.* He says the room will be ready in twenty minutes but I doubt it.

doux, douce sweet *J'adore les marrons glacés mais ils sont très doux.* I love candied chestnuts but they are very sweet.

douzaine *f.* dozen *J'y suis allé une douzaine de fois.* I've been there a dozen times.

drap *m.* sheet *Il faut demander des draps propres.* We must ask for clean sheets.

drapeau *m.*   flag   *Le drapeau français est bleu, blanc, et rouge.*   The French flag is blue, white, and red.

droit   straight   *Allez tout droit et vous verrez la banque.*   Go straight ahead and you will see the bank.

droite *f.*   right   *Le bureau de poste est à droite.*   The post office is to the right.

dur   hard, difficult, harsh   *Son enfance était dure.*   His childhood was harsh.

durer   to last   *Le règne de Louis XIV a duré soixante-douze ans.*   The reign of Louis XIV lasted seventy-two years.

eau *f.*   water   *En France, dans les restaurants, on boit de l'eau minérale, en général.*   In France, mineral water usually is drunk in restaurants.

échanger   to exchange   *J'aimerais échanger cette robe que j'ai achetée hier.*   I would like to exchange this dress that I bought yesterday.

échouer   to fail   *Il a échoué à l'examen.*   He failed the exam.

école *f.*   school   *Les écoles sont fermées pour Noël.*   Schools are closed for Christmas.

écouter   to listen to   *Il écoute les nouvelles à la radio.*   He is listening to the news on the radio.

écrire   to write   *Il écrit chaque jour dans son journal.*   He writes in his diary every day.

écriteau *m.*   sign, notice   *L'écriteau dit: "Fermé le lundi."*   The sign says: "Closed on Mondays."

effet *m.*   effect   *En effet, c'est une belle surprise de vous voir ici.*   In fact, it's a great surprise to see you here.

effort *m.*   effort   *Il a soulevé le poids sans effort.*   He lifted the weight without effort.

égal   equal, same   *Cela lui est égal.*   It's all the same to him.

également   equally, likewise   *En France, les femmes ont obtenu beaucoup de droits; également, cela est arrivé aux Etats-Unis.*   In France, women have gained many rights; likewise, that has happened in the United States.

église *f.*   church   *Il y a une église catholique très près d'ici.*   There is a Catholic church very near here.

elle *f.*   she   *Elle est partie.*   She left.

embassade *f.*   embassy   *Les embassades de tous les pays étrangers sont à Paris.*   The embassies of all the foreign countries are in Paris.

embrasser   to embrace, hug, kiss   *Elle a embrassé ses parents avant de partir.*   She hugged her parents before she left.

emploi *m.*   employment, job   *Je cherche un emploi près de chez moi.*   I am looking for a job near my house.

employé(e) employee *Les employés d'Air France étaient en grève l'été passé.* The employees of Air France were on strike last summer.

enchanté delighted, enchanted *Enchanté de faire votre connaissance.* Delighted to meet you.

encore still, again, yet *Elle n'a pas encore fait ses devoirs.* She hasn't done her homework yet.

encre *f.* ink *Ecrivez à l'encre.* Write in ink.

endroit *m.* place, spot *C'est un endroit parfait pour notre pique-nique.* It's a perfect spot for our picnic.

enfant *m./f.* child, kid *Les enfants font trop de bruit.* The kids are making too much noise.

enlever to take away, to take off *Enlevez les livres de la table, s'il vous plaît.* Take the books away from the table, please.

ennui *m.* bother *C'est un grand ennui de devoir faire cela.* It's a great bother to have to do that.

ennuyer to annoy, bore *Il m'ennuie toujours avec ses plaintes.* He is always annoying me with his complaints.

enseigner to teach *Il m'a enseigné à conduire.* He taught me how to drive.

ensemble together *Nous pouvons voyager ensemble.* We can travel together.

ensuite then, next, after *Nous avons déjeuné ensemble et ensuite nous avons causé pendant une heure.* We ate lunch together and then we chatted for an hour.

entendre to hear; to understand *On entend le bruit du train pendant la nuit.* We hear the noise of the train during the night. *Alors, c'est entendu.* So, it's understood.

entendu, bien of course *Bien entendu nous irons avec vous.* Of course we'll go with you.

entracte *m.* intermission, interval *On causera encore pendant l'entracte.* We'll chat some more during intermission.

entre between, among *Entre nous, ce n'est pas une bonne idée d'aller le voir à l'hôpital.* Between us, it's not a good idea to go see him at the hospital.

entrée *f.* entrance, admission *L'entrée est gratuite le dimanche.* Admission is free on Sundays.

entrer to enter, come in *Frappez à la porte avant d'entrer.* Knock at the door before entering.

enveloppe *f.* envelope *J'ai trouvé une enveloppe pour ma lettre.* I found an envelope for my letter.

envelopper to wrap *J'ai enveloppé ces verres de sorte qu'ils ne se casseront pas.* I have wrapped these glasses so that they will not break.

envie *f.*   desire   *Je n'ai pas envie d'aller au cinéma ce soir.*   I don't feel like going to the movies tonight.

envoyer   to send   *Je désire envoyer des cartes postales à mes amis aux Etats-Unis.*   I want to send some postcards to my friends in the United States.

épaule *f.*   shoulder   *Il a mal à l'épaule parce qu'il a porté une valise très lourde.*   His shoulder hurts because he carried a very heavy suitcase.

épicé   spicy   *Les plats de la cuisine créole sont plutôt épicés.*   Creole cookery is rather spicy.

équipe *f.*   team   *L'équipe de football de ton frère a gagné la partie et est en train de célébrer.*   Your brother's soccer team won the game and is celebrating right now.

escalier *m.*   stairs, staircase   *Si vous montez l'escalier et tournez à droite vous trouverez votre chambre.*   If you go upstairs and turn right you will find your room.

espace *m.*   space   *Il faut avoir assez d'espace entre vous et la voiture devant vous.*   There must be enough space between you and the car in front of you.

Espagne *f.*   Spain   *Nous sommes allés de France en Espagne en traversant les Pyrénées.*   We went from France to Spain by crossing the Pyrenees.

espagnol *m.*   Spanish   *Avant d'aller au Mexique j'ai étudié l'espagnol.*   Before going to Mexico I studied Spanish.

espérer   to hope   *J'espère te revoir un jour.*   I hope to see you again some day.

essayer   to try, to taste   *Essayez cette crêpe et dites-moi si elle vous plaît.*   Try this pancake and tell me if you like it.

est *m.*   east   *La Suisse est le pays à l'est de la France.*   Switzerland is the country to the east of France.

estomac *m.*   stomach   *Nous avons tous mal à l'estomac.*   We all have a stomachache.

et   and   *Lui et moi, nous viendrons ensemble.*   He and I will come together.

étage *m.*   story, floor   *Cet édifice a sept étages.*   This building has seven floors.

état *m.*   state, condition   *L'état du Texas a à peu près les mêmes dimensions que la France.*   The state of Texas is almost the same size as France.

Etats-Unis *m. pl.*   United States   *Dans l'état de Louisiane aux Etats-Unis beaucoup de gens parlent encore français.*   In the state of Louisiana in the United States many people still speak French.

éteindre   to turn off, extinguish   *Il faut éteindre la lumière avant de sortir.*   You must turn off the light before you go out.

étoffe *f.*   cloth, fabric   *C'est une belle étoffe.*   It's a beautiful fabric.

étoile *f.*   star   *Les étoiles brillent dans le ciel.*   The stars are shining in the sky.

étrange   strange   *C'est étrange que nos amis ne soient pas ici.*   It's strange that our friends are not here.

étranger *m.*   foreigner; stranger   *C'est un étranger qui ne parle pas français.*   He is a foreigner who does not speak French.

être   to be   *Quelle est ta valise?*   Which is your suitcase?

étroit   narrow, tight   *La porte au jardin est très étroite.*   The door to the garden is very narrow.

étudiant(e)   student   *Les étudiants de la Sorbonne se trouvent dans les cafés.*   The Sorbonne students meet in the cafés.

étudier   to study   *Avant d'aller en France mon fils va étudier le français.*   Before going to France my son is going to study French.

Europe *f.*   Europe   *La Communauté européenne unit beaucoup des pays d'Europe avec un seul passeport.*   The European Community unites many of the countries of Europe with a single passport.

évanouir, s'   to faint   *Quand elle a entendu la mauvaise nouvelle, elle s'est évanouie.*   When she heard the bad news, she fainted.

évantail *m.*   fan   *Cette dame a un évantail parce qu'il fait chaud.*   That lady has a fan because it is hot.

examen *m.*   exam   *Notre professeur a annoncé un examen pour la semaine prochaine.*   Our teacher announced an exam for next week.

exemplaire *m.*   sample   *Voici un exemplaire du travail d'un de nos ouvriers.*   Here is a sample of the work of one of our workmen.

exemple *m.*   example   *Ceci est un exemple de sa traduction.*   This is an example of his translation.

exiger   to demand, to require   *Il exige que les exercices de laboratoire soient remis avant l'examen final.*   He requires that the laboratory exercises be handed in before the final exam.

expliquer   to explain   *Il a expliqué qu'il n'avait pas écrit parce qu'il avait perdu notre adresse.*   He explained that he hadn't written because he had lost our address.

face (en __ de)   opposite, facing   *En face de nous, nous voyons l'Hôtel de ville.*   Facing us, we see City Hall.

facile   easy   *Ces exercices de français ne sont pas faciles.*   These French exercises are not easy.

faible   weak   *Il se sent faible après sa maladie.*   He feels weak after his illness.

faim *f.*   hunger   *Nous avons une faim de loup.*   We are hungry as a wolf.

faire   to do, make   *Nous avons beaucoup d'achats à faire.*   We have many purchases to make.

famille *f.*   family   *Elle va tous les étés chez sa famille en France.*   She goes to her family's home in France every summer.

fatigué   tired   *Je suis fatigué après cette longue promenade.*   I am tired after that long walk.

faute *f.*   mistake   *Il y a des fautes de grammaire dans cette composition.* There are grammar mistakes in this composition.

félicitations *f. pl.*   congratulations   *Mes félicitations pour la naissance de votre fils.*   Congratulations on the birth of your son.

femme *f.*   woman; wife   *Cette jeune femme est sans abri.*   This young woman is homeless.

femme de chambre *f.*   chambermaid   *La femme de chambre vous apportera du savon.*   The chambermaid will bring you some soap.

fenêtre *f.*   window   *Les fenêtres de ma chambre donnent sur la cour.* The windows of my bedroom face the courtyard.

fermé   closed   *Le lundi beaucoup de musées sont fermés.*   Many museums are closed on Mondays.

fermer   to close   *Fermez la porte, s'il vous plaît.*   Close the door, please.

fête *f.*   holiday, celebration   *Le quatorze juillet est la fête nationale française.*   July fourteenth is the French national holiday.

feu   fire, (traffic) light   *Il ne faut pas traverser s'il y a le feu rouge.*   You must not cross if there is a red light.

fiancé(e) *m./f.*   fiancé(e), boyfriend, girlfriend   *Mon fils aime sa jeune fiancée.*   My son loves his young fiancée.

fier à, se   to trust   *Il faut se fier à notre guide.*   We must trust our guide.

fièvre *f.*   fever   *Tu as mal à la gorge et de la fièvre. Ne sorte pas.*   You have a sore throat and fever. Don't go out.

figure *f.*   face   *Elle a la figure très jolie.*   She has a very pretty face.

fil, un coup de *m.*   call, ring   *Donne-moi un coup de fil demain.*   Give me a call tomorrow.

fin *f.*   end   *La fin de l'été est ici.*   The end of the summer is here.

finir   to finish   *Il finit ses devoirs avant de se coucher.*   He finishes his homework before going to bed.

fleur *f.*   flower   *J'ai envoyé des fleurs à la mère du bébé.*   I sent flowers to the baby's mother.

fleuve *m.* (**rivière** *f.*)   river   *La Loire est le plus long des fleuves de France.*   The Loire is the longest river in France.

foi *f.*   faith   *Le chef du gouvernement doit inspirer la foi du peuple.* The head of the government must inspire the faith of the people.

fois *f.*   time (occasion)   *Une fois ne suffit pas.*   Once is not enough.

fonctionner   to work, function   *Cet ordinateur fonctionne bien maintenant.*   This computer works well now.

football *m.*   soccer   *Le football est le sport favori des Français.*   Soccer is the favorite sport of the French.

fort   strong   *Ce porteur de bagage est très fort.*   This luggage porter is very strong.

fou, folle   crazy, insane, mad   *Tu es fou si tu continues à travailler dans ce lieu.*   You are crazy if you continue to work in that place.

fourchette *f.*   fork   *Apportez-moi une autre fourchette, je vous en prie.*   Bring me another fork, please.

français *m.*   French   *Il enseigne le français à New York.*   He teaches French in New York.

France *f.*   France   *La France est séparée de l'Italie par les Alpes.*   France is separated from Italy by the Alps.

frit(es)   fried   *Des pommes frites, s'il vous plaît.*   Some French fries, please.

froid   cold   *Le potage est froid.*   The soup is cold.

front *m.*   forehead; (military) front   *Il a frappé la front contre la branche d'un arbre.*   He hit his forehead against the branch of a tree.

frontière *f.*   border   *A la frontière, il faut montrer son passeport.*   At the border you have to show your passport.

fumée *f.*   smoke   *On voyait la fumée de l'incendie de forêt de très loin.*   The smoke from the forest fire was seen from very far away.

fumer   to smoke   *J'ai conseillé à mes élèves de ne pas fumer.*   I advised my pupils not to smoke.

fur *m.*, **au, et à mesure**   progressively, gradually   *Au fur et à mesure qu'ils marchaient et couraient ensemble, sa tristesse a disparu.*   Gradually, as they walked and ran together, her sadness disappeared.

gagner   to earn, win   *Il gagne beaucoup d'argent.*   He earns a lot of money.

gant *m.*   glove   *N'oublie pas tes gants, il fait froid.*   Don't forget your gloves—it's cold.

garçon *m.*   boy, waiter   *Garçon, l'addition s'il vous plaît.*   Waiter, the check, please.

garde *m./f.*   guard, watchman   *Le garde de nuit a un chien-loup.*   The night watchman has a police dog.

gare *f.*   railroad station   *Vous pouvez trouver un taxi à la gare.*   You can find a taxi at the railroad station.

garer   to park   *On peut garer la voiture devant la maison sauf le jeudi de dix heures à quatorze heures.*   You can park the car in front of the house except Thursdays from 10:00 A.M. to 2:00 P.M.

gauche   left   *Au carrefour, tournez à gauche.*   At the crossroads, turn left.

genou(x) *m.* knee(s) *A l'église beaucoup de gens se mettent à genoux pour prier.* In church many people get on their knees to pray.

gens *m. pl.* people *Il y avait beaucoup de gens à Giverny pour voir la maison et les jardins de Monet.* There were many people at Giverny to see Monet's house and gardens.

gérant *m.* manager *Il est devenu le gérant de l'entreprise.* He has become the manager of the business.

glace *f.* mirror, ice, ice cream *On voyait la mer reflétée dans la glace du restaurant.* We saw the sea reflected in the mirror of the restaurant. *J'aimerais une glace au chocolat.* I would like a chocolate ice cream.

gorge *f.* throat *Je vais prendre deux aspirines avant de me coucher parce que j'ai mal à la gorge.* I'm going to take two aspirins before going to bed because I have a sore throat.

goûter *m.* afternoon snack *Les enfants prennent le goûter après l'école.* Children have a snack after school.

goutte *f.* drop *Il a bu la dernière goutte d'eau.* He drank the last drop of water.

gouvernement *m.* government *Le premier ministre est le chef du gouvernement de France.* The prime minister is the head of the government of France.

grand tall, large; great *Charles de Gaulle était un grand homme et aussi un homme grand.* Charles de Gaulle was a great man and also a tall man.

grand magasin *m.* department store *Je cherche un grand magasin pour faire mes achats.* I'm looking for a department store to make my purchases.

grève *f.* strike *Les pilotes d'Air France sont allés en grève.* The pilots of Air France went on strike.

gros (grosse) fat *Elle doit suivre un régime parce qu'elle est trop grosse.* She must go on a diet because she is too fat.

groupe *m.* group *Il y a trente étudiants dans le groupe des commençants.* There are thirty students in the beginner's group.

guerre *f.* war *La guerre entre la France et l'Angleterre a duré cent ans.* The war between France and England lasted one hundred years.

guichet *m.* ticket office *Il y a une queue au guichet.* There is a line at the ticket office.

guide *m.* guide; guidebook *Notre guide nous a montré tous les aspects intéressants de Chartres.* Our guide showed us all the interesting aspects of Chartres.

habiller, s' to get dressed *Je me suis habillé de bonne heure mais les ouvriers ne sont pas encore arrivés.* I got dressed early but the workmen have not yet arrived.

haïr   to hate   *Il y a des gens qui haïssent l'idée de la Communauté européenne.*   There are some people who hate the idea of the European Community.

hasard *m.*   chance, coincidence   *Connaissez-vous, par hasard, le professeur Arditty?*   Do you know Professor Arditty by any chance?

haut   tall, high   *La Tour Eiffel est très haute.*   The Eiffel Tower is very tall.

haut, en   upstairs, above   *La salle de bains est en haut.*   The bathroom is upstairs.

heure *f.*   hour; time   *Quelle heure est-il?*   What time is it?

heureux (euse)   happy   *Que je suis heureux!*   How happy I am!

hier   yesterday   *Hier je me suis fatigué et j'ai besoin de me reposer.*   Yesterday I got tired out and I need to rest.

homme *m.*   man   *Les hommes et les femmes de cette université participent beaucoup aux sports.*   The men and women of that university take part in sports a lot.

homme/femme d'affaires *m./f.*   businessman/ -woman   *Les hommes d'affaires vont souvent à ce restaurant.*   Businessmen often go to this restaurant.

honte *f.*   shame   *J'ai honte d'avouer que le travail n'est pas terminé.*   I am ashamed to say that the job is not finished.

horaire *m.*   schedule, timetable   *Voici l'horaire des trains de Paris à Lyon.*   Here is the Paris–Lyon train schedule.

hors (de)   outside   *Cette ligne d'autobus va hors de la ville.*   This bus line goes out of the city.

hôtel de ville *m.*   city hall, town hall   *Ils vont se marier dans l'hôtel de ville.*   They are going to get married in the town hall.

ici   here   *Ici on vend les timbres.*   Stamps are sold here.

il *m.*   he   *Il est parti.*   He left.

il y a   there is, there are   *Il y a tellement de beaux musées at de beaux monuments à voir que je ne sais pas où commencer.*   There are so many beautiful museums and beautiful monuments to see that I don't know where to begin.

ils *m.* **(elles** *f.*)   they   *Je pense qu'ils nous suivront.*   I think that they will follow us.

immédiatement   immediately   *Descends du train immédiatement.*   Get off the train immediately.

imperméable *m.*   raincoat   *Mettez votre imperméable parce qu'il pleut déjà.*   Wear your raincoat because it's already raining.

importer   to matter, to be important   *Qu'importe?*   What does it matter?

impôt *m.*   tax   *On a augmenté les impôts sur les parfums français aux*

Etats-Unis.   Taxes on French perfumes have been increased in the United States.

incendie *m.*   fire   *C'était un incendie criminel.*   It was a fire by arson.

indiquer   to indicate, show   *Voulez-vous bien m'indiquer où se trouve la Banque de France?*   Would you please show me where the Banque de France is located?

ingénieur *m.*   engineer   *Mon père était ingénieur.*   My father was an engineer.

inquiéter, s'   to worry   *Ne vous inquiétez pas!*   Don't worry!

intérêt *m.*   interest   *La Bibliothèque nationale est sans doute un des points d'intérêt.*   The National Library is undoubtedly one of the points of interest.

intérieur *m.*   inside, interior   *Il est plus confortable ici, à l'intérieur.*   It's more comfortable here inside.

inutile   useless   *Il est inutile de faire une grève maintenant.*   It is useless to go on strike now.

invité(e) *m./f.*   guest   *Elle avait quatre invités à dîner.*   She had four guests for dinner.

ivre   drunk   *Ce monsieur est tout à fait ivre.*   That man is completely drunk.

jamais   ever, never   *Avez-vous jamais mangé les huîtres?*   Have you ever eaten oysters?   *Jamais.*   Never.

jamais, ne   never   *Je n'ai jamais visité Sète, où Valéry a écrit "Le Cimetière marin."*   I never have visited Sète, where Valéry wrote "The Cemetery by the Sea."

jambe *f.*   leg   *J'ai mal à la jambe droite.*   My right leg hurts.

jardin *m.*   garden   *Visitez le Jardin du Luxembourg!*   Visit the Luxembourg Gardens!

je   I   *Je suis très impatiente de savoir la nouvelle.*   I am very impatient to hear the news.

jeter   to throw, throw away   *Ne jetez pas la balle près des fenêtres.*   Don't throw the ball near the windows.   *Ne jetez pas ce journal. Je ne l'ai pas encore lu.*   Do not throw away this newspaper. I have not read it yet.

jeu *m.*   game   *Le jeu d'échecs exige beaucoup de concentration et de maîtrise.*   The game of chess requires much concentration and expertise.

jeune   young   *A son jeune âge, il a déjà beaucoup accompli.*   At his young age, he has already accomplished a lot.

joli(e)   pretty   *Ta nouvelle robe est très jolie.*   Your new dress is very pretty.

jouer   to play   *Qui va jouer au tennis?*   Who is going to play tennis?

jouet *m.* toy *Les enfants ont trop de jouets aujourd'hui.* Children have too many toys today.

jouir de to enjoy *Ils jouissent d'une vie saine à la campagne.* They are enjoying a healthy life in the country.

jour *m.* day *Quel jour sommes-nous aujourd'hui?* What day is it today?/ What is today's date?

journal *m.* newspaper *Je sors pour acheter le journal.* I am going out to buy the newspaper.

juge *m.* judge *À ce procès, le juge est très respecté.* At this trial, the judge is very respected.

Juif (ve) Jew *C'est un Juif italien qui habite en France depuis longtemps.* He is an Italian Jew who has lived in France for a long time.

jupe *f.* skirt *On porte les jupes courtes ou longues comme on préfère cette année.* Skirts are worn short or long as one prefers this year.

jurer to swear *Ils ont juré de dire la vérité au procès.* They swore to tell the truth at the trial.

jusqu'à until *Il a dormi jusqu'à dix heures.* He slept until ten o'clock.

kilo(gramme) *m.* kilo(gram) (2.2 lbs.) *Les pêches coûtent douze francs le kilo.* The peaches cost twelve francs a kilo.

kilomètre *m.* kilometer (5/8 of a mile) *On peut aller à cent kilomètres à l'heure sur l'autoroute.* You can go one hundred kilometers an hour on the highway.

la *f.* the; her; it *On a sonné à la porte; c'est la bonne.* Someone rang the doorbell; it's the maid. *Vous la trouverez très aimable.* You will find her very nice.

là there *J'aimerais dîner là.* I would like to eat there.

lac *m.* lake *Il y a un grand lac à Honfleur, près de Paris.* There is a big lake in Honfleur, near Paris.

laid ugly *Ce chien est vraiment laid.* That dog is really ugly.

laine *f.* wool *On fait des chandails magnifiques de la laine des moutons français.* Magnificent sweaters are made from the wool of French sheep.

laisser to let, permit, allow, leave *On ne laisse entrer personne sans permission spéciale.* They don't let anyone enter without special permission.

lampe *f.* lamp *Tout le long de la Seine il y a des lampes.* All along the Seine, there are lamps.

langue *f.* tongue, language *Mon bureau est dans le Département de langues étrangères.* My office is in the Foreign Languages Department.

large wide *Les rues principales sont larges et belles.* The main streets are wide and beautiful.

lavabo *m.* sink, lavatory *Je cherche les lavabos.* I am looking for the lavatories.

laver, se to wash (oneself) *Il faut laver le plancher.* We must wash the floor.

le *m.;* **la** *f.* the, it, him, her *Le guide et les touristes américains vont visiter les châteaux de la Loire.* The guide and the American tourists are going to visit the castles of the Loire valley. *Je la vois tous les jours.* I see her every day.

leçon *f.* lesson *La leçon sur les verbes réfléchis est toujours difficile pour les étudiants.* The lesson on reflexive verbs is always difficult for the students.

léger, -ère light (weight) *Un imperméable léger est idéal pour le voyage.* A light raincoat is ideal for the trip.

lentement slowly *Parlez plus lentement, je vous en prie.* Speak more slowly, please.

lequel which, which one *Lequel apportez-vous?* Which one are you bringing?

les *m./f. pl.* the, them *Ces enfants ont jeté les miettes de pain aux canards; je les ai vus.* These children threw the bread crumbs to the ducks; I saw them.

lettre *f.* letter *J'ai enfin reçu une lettre de mon ami en France.* I have finally received a letter from my friend in France.

lever to lift, raise *Levez la main si vous avez fini la composition.* Raise your hand if you have finished the composition.

lèvre *f.* lip *Elle a les lèvres à Cupidon.* She has Cupid lips.

libre free *Après l'université, elle était libre de choisir son sort.* After the university, she was free to choose her destiny.

lieu *m.* place *Je connais un lieu qui est très agréable.* I know a place that is very pleasant.

ligne *f.* line *Commencez à lire à la ligne treize.* Start reading on line thirteen.

limite *f.* limit *Quelle est la limite de vitesse ici?* What is the speed limit here?

lire to read *J'aime lire avant de m'endormir.* I like to read before going to sleep.

liste *f.* list *Voici une liste de restaurants à prix modéré.* Here is a list of moderately priced restaurants.

lit *m.* bed *Je désire une chambre à deux lits.* I want a room with two beds.

litre *m.* liter (1.06 quarts) *Un litre de lait et une douzaine d'oeufs, s'il vous plaît.* A liter of milk and a dozen eggs, please.

livre *m.* book *J'ai des livres que j'ai relus plusieurs fois.* I have books that I have reread several times.

loi *f.* law *Si vous traversez au feu rouge, c'est contre la loi.* If you cross with a red light, it's against the law.

loin far (away) *La gare est loin d'ici.* The railroad station is far from here.

long, longue long *Nous avons fait une longue promenade.* We took a long walk.

louer to rent *Je désire louer une voiture pour mon voyage.* I want to rent a car for my trip.

lourd(e) heavy *Votre valise est trop lourde.* Your suitcase is too heavy.

lui to him, to her *Je lui ai dit de venir nous faire visite.* I told him (her) to come visit us.

lumière *f.* light *C'était romantique de marcher à la lumière de la lune.* It was romantic to walk in the moonlight.

lune *f.* moon *La lune était la seule lumière dans la montagne cette nuit.* The moon was the only light in the mountains that night.

lunettes *f. pl.* eyeglasses *Il ne peut pas conduire sans lunettes.* He cannot drive without eyeglasses.

lutte *f.* struggle, fight *La lutte entre père et fils a duré longtemps.* The struggle between father and son lasted a long time.

luxe *m.* luxury *C'est une croisière de luxe.* It is a luxury cruise.

madame *f.* Mrs.; lady *Madame Paule est mon prof de mathématiques.* Mrs. Paule is my math professor.

mademoiselle *f.* young lady, Miss *Est-ce que mademoiselle Dupont est absente aujourd'hui?* Is Miss Dupont absent today?

magasin *m.* store, shop *Je cherche un magasin de bijouterie.* I am looking for a jewelry store.

magnétophone *m.* tape recorder *J'ai besoin d'un magnétophone pour écouter mes cassettes.* I need a tape recorder to listen to my tapes.

magnétoscope *m.* VCR *J'ai acheté deux vidéocassettes pour le nouveau magnétoscope.* I bought two video tapes for the new VCR.

main *f.* hand *Donne-moi la main.* Give me your hand.

maintenant now *Je ne peux pas vous aider maintenant.* I can't help you now.

maire *m.* mayor *C'est le maire qui va marier les deux jeunes personnes.* It's the mayor who will perform the marriage of the two young people.

mais but *Nous sommes allés voir le Musée de l'Homme mais il est fermé le mardi.* We went to see the Museum of Humankind but it is closed on Tuesdays.

maison *f.* house, home   *Il y a de jolies maisons dans ce quartier.* There are pretty homes in this neighborhood.

maître (-esse) master, teacher   *Les maîtres d'école doivent avoir beaucoup de patience avec les enfants.*   Schoolteachers must have a lot of patience with the children.

mal *m.* evil; hurt, pain   *Il s'est fait mal quand il est tombé.*   He hurt himself when he fell.

mal avoir to hurt to ache   *J'ai mal à la tête.*   I have a headache.

malade sick, ill   *Il est absent de l'école parce qu'il est malade.*   He is absent from school because he is ill.

malheur *m.* misfortune   *Quel malheur que votre père est mort, mon enfant. Par malheur, je ne peux rien faire pour vous aider.*   What a misfortune that your father has died, my child. Unfortunately, I can do nothing to help you.

malle *f.* trunk   *Il est arrivé avec une malle pleine de livres.*   He arrived with a trunk full of books.

manger to eat   *On mange bien en France.*   You eat well in France.

manière *f.* manner, way   *Il explique les choses d'une manière très claire.* He explains things in a very clear way.

manquer to miss; to lack   *Il a manqué la classe.*   He missed class. *Son père lui manque.*   She misses her father.

manteau *m.* coat   *On porte un manteau parce qu'il fait froid ici.*   We are wearing a coat because it's cold here.

marché *m.* market   *Il achète le tabac au marché noir.*   He buys the tobacco at the black market.

marcher to walk, to march   *Vous marchez vite!*   You walk quickly!

mariage *m.* wedding   *La fête du mariage aura lieu à Montmartre.* The wedding reception will take place in Montmartre.

marié married   *Son fils aîné n'est pas marié.*   Her oldest son is not married.

marier, se to get married   *Il s'est marié avec une jeune fille plus âgée que lui.*   He married a girl older than he.

match *m.* game   *Aimeriez-vous aller à un match de football?*   Would you like to go to a soccer game?

mauvais bad   *Il fait mauvais temps aujourd'hui.*   The weather is bad today.

me (to) me   *Il me dit toujours de conduire avec prudence.*   He always tells me to drive cautiously. *Il m'aime bien.*   He likes me.

médecin *m.* doctor, physician   *Il faut appeler le médecin parce que je suis malade.*   We must call the doctor because I am sick.

meilleur better, best   *Cet hôtel est meilleur que l'autre.*   This hotel is better than the other one. *C'est le meilleur hôtel de cette ville.*   It's the best hotel in this town.

membre *m.* member *Elle est membre de notre société.* She is a member of our society.

même same, very *Le jour même j'ai rencontré la même personne.* On that very day I met the same person.

mensonge *m.* lie *Ne la croyez pas; elle dit des mensonges.* Don't believe her; she tells lies.

mer *f.* sea *Nous allons au bord de la mer en été.* We go to the seashore in the summer.

merci thanks *Merci de votre gentillesse.* Thank you for your kindness.

mériter to deserve *Ce jeune homme mérite une augmentation de salaire.* That young man deserves a raise in his wages.

message *m.* message *J'ai reçu un message électronique.* I received an email message.

méthode *f.* method *Il faut trouver une méthode plus efficace.* We must find a more efficient method.

mètre *m.* meter (1.1 yards) *Il y a mille mètres dans un kilomètre.* There are a thousand meters in a kilometer.

mettre to put, put on, place *Ne mettez pas vos affaires sur la table à manger.* Don't put your belongings on the dining-room table.

meubles *m. pl.* furniture *Nous avons acheté de nouveaux meubles.* We bought new furniture.

midi *m.* noon *Nous déjeunons à midi d'habitude.* We have lunch at noon, usually.

mien, mienne mine *Ce livre est à toi. Ce n'est pas le mien.* This book belongs to you. It is not mine.

mille *m.* mile; thousand *Combien de kilomètres y a-t-il en six milles?* How many kilometers are there in six miles?

mince thin, slim, slender *Si tu veux être mince, suis ce régime.* If you want to be slim, follow this diet.

minuit *m.* midnight *Quand Cendrillon a entendu sonner minuit, elle est partie tout de suite.* When Cinderella heard midnight sounding, she left immediately.

miracle *m.* miracle *C'est un miracle qu'il ait survécu l'ouragan.* It's a miracle that he survived the hurricane.

mode *f.* style, fashion *Ce chapeau est très à la mode.* That hat is very much in fashion.

moindre lesser, lower; le __ least, slightest *Il n'a le moindre soupçon.* He hasn't the slightest suspicion.

moins less; le __ least *Ce restaurant est moins cher.* This restaurant is less expensive.

mois *m.* month *En quel mois préférez-vous voyager?* In which month do you prefer to travel?

moitié *f.*   half   *Je te donnerai la moitié de ma glace.*   I will give you half of my ice cream.

mon, ma, mes   my   *J'aimerais vous présenter mon mari et mes fils.*   I would like to introduce my husband and my sons to you.

monde *m.*   world   *Le monde semble devenir plus petit.*   The world seems to get smaller.

monnaie *f.*   change; coin   *Il m'a rendu la monnaie.*   He gave me back the change.   *Pardon, mais je n'ai pas de monnaie.*   Excuse me, but I have no change.

monsieur *m.*   Mr., sir, gentleman   *Merci, monsieur, de votre gentillesse.*   Thank you, sir, for your kindness.

montagne *f.*   mountain   *Allons à la montagne!*   Let's go to the mountains!

monter   to go up   *Je dois monter à notre chambre et j'ai oublié ma clé.*   I have to go up to our room and I forgot my key.

montre *f.*   watch   *Ma montre avance de deux minutes.*   My watch is two minutes fast.

montrer   to show   *Montrez-moi votre petit chat.*   Show me your little cat.

morceau *m.*   piece   *Le mendiant demande un morceau de pain.*   The beggar is asking for a piece of bread.

mort   dead   *Je suis morte de fatigue.*   I am dead tired.

mort *f.*   death   *La mort de son mari l'a bouleversée complètement.*   The death of her husband completely overwhelmed her.

mot *m.*   word   *C'est un nouveau mot pour vous.*   It's a new word for you.

moto *f.*   (motocyclette) motorbike, motorcycle   *En France beaucoup de jeunes gens ont une moto.*   In France many young people have motorcycles.

mouchoir *m.*   handkerchief   *Je vais acheter une douzaine de mouchoirs blancs de coton.*   I am going to buy a dozen white cotton handkerchiefs.

mouillé (e)   wet   *Il est arrivé tout mouillé de la pluie.*   He arrived all wet from the rain.

mourir   to die   *Ce professeur est mort l'année dernière.*   That professor died last year.

moyen *m.*   way, manner, means   *J'ai trouvé le moyen de ne pas l'offenser.*   I found the way not to offend him.

mur *m.*   wall   *Accrochez le miroir au mur.*   Hang the mirror on the wall.

mûr   ripe   *En Septembre le raisin est mûr.*   In September the grapes are ripe.

musée *m.*   museum   *Le musée Rodin à Paris est magnifique.*   The Rodin museum in Paris is magnificent.

musique *f.*   music   *La musique des concerts de la Sainte-Chapelle est extra-ordinaire.*   The music of the Sainte-Chapelle concerts is extraordinary.

nager   to swim   *Je vais nager dans la piscine.*   I am going to swim in the pool.

naître   to be born   *Le petit bébé est né hier.*   The little baby was born yesterday.

ne __ ni __ ni __   neither, nor   *Il ne mange ni viande ni poisson.*   He eats neither meat nor fish.

néanmoins   nevertheless   *Néanmoins, je désire la voir.*   Nevertheless, I want to see her.

nécessaire   necessary   *Il n'est pas nécessaire d'apporter un cadeau.*   It is not necessary to bring a gift.

neige *f.*   snow   *Il y a beaucoup de neige à Chamonix l'hiver et on y fait du ski.*   There is a lot of snow in Chamonix in the winter and people go skiing there.

neiger   to snow   *Il neige toujours dans les Alpes.*   It always snows in the Alps.

nettoyer   to clean   *Ils doivent nettoyer la chambre.*   They have to clean the room.

nez *m.*   nose   *Cyrano avait un très grand nez.*   Cyrano had a very large nose.

nier   to deny   *Il a nié d'avoir laissé la porte ouverte.*   He denied leaving the door open.

niveau *m.*   level   *Nous sommes au niveau de la mer ici.*   We are at sea level here.

Noël *m.*   Christmas   *Joyeux Noël!*   Merry Christmas!

nom *m.*   name   *Son nom est Michel.*   His name is Michael.

nom de famille *m.*   surname   *Quel est votre nom de famille?*   What is your surname?

non   no   *Non, je n'aime pas le homard.*   No, I don't like lobster.

non plus, ni __   neither   *Il n'a pas vu l'accident. Ni moi non plus.*   He didn't see the accident. Nor did I.

nord *m.*   north   *Amiens est au nord de Paris.*   Amiens is north of Paris.

notre   our   *Notre guide connaît l'histoire de tous ces lieux.*   Our guide knows the history of all these places.

nous   we, us, to us   *Nous allons visiter Versailles.*   We are going to visit Versailles.   *Le guide nous accompagnera.*   The guide will accompany us.   *Elle nous a demandé d'aller dîner chez elle après.*   She asked us to have dinner at her house afterward.

nouveau   new   *Quoi de nouveau?*   What's new?

nouvelle *f.*   news, piece of news   *Il nous a donné la nouvelle que son fils s'était fiancé.*   He gave us the news that his son was engaged.

nuage *m.*   cloud   *Un nuage cache le soleil.*   A cloud is hiding the sun.

nuageux   cloudy   *Il est très nuageux; je crois qu'il va pleuvoir.*   It's very cloudy; I think it's going to rain.

nuit *f.*   night   *La nuit, cette rue est très tranquille.*   At night, this street is very peaceful.

numéro *m.*   number   *Voici mon numéro de téléphone.*   Here is my phone number.

objet *m.*   object, purpose   *Quel est l'objet de ton voyage?*   What is the purpose of your trip?

obliger   to oblige, force   *On a été obligé de faire un détour.*   We were obliged to make a detour.

obtenir   to obtain   *Où pouvons-nous obtenir un carnet de billets de métro?*   Where can we obtain a book of metro tickets?

occasion *f.*   occasion, opportunity; bargain   *Ne perds pas l'occasion de faire ce voyage!*   Don't miss the opportunity of taking this trip! *Cette voiture était très bon marché, une véritable occasion.*   This car was very inexpensive, a true bargain.

occupé   busy, occupied   *Je suis très occupé aujourd'hui, mais demain j'aimerais bien déjeuner avec toi.*   I am very busy today, but tomorrow I should like very much to have lunch with you.

océan *m.*   ocean   *L'océan Atlantique sépare la France des Etats-Unis.*   The Atlantic Ocean divides France from the United States.

odeur *f.*   odor, smell   *On sent une odeur de tabac dans cette chambre.*   We can smell an odor of tobacco in this bedroom.

oeil *m.*   eye   *Il est aveugle d'un oeil.*   He is blind in one eye.

oeuvre *f.*   work   *Il y a des oeuvres de Daumier dans ce musée.*   There are some of Daumier's works in this museum.

ombre *f.*   shade, shadow   *Stationnez la voiture à l'ombre.*   Park the car in the shade.

once *f.*   ounce   *Il faut avoir deux onces de vanille pour faire ce gâteau.*   We must have two ounces of vanilla to make this cake.

or *m.*   gold   *Cette bague d'or appartenait à ma mère.*   That gold ring belonged to my mother.

ordinateur *m.*   computer   *Beaucoup d'enfants apprennent à utiliser un ordinateur même avant d'entrer à l'école.*   Many children learn to use a computer even before entering school.

ordonnance *f.*   prescription.   *Mon ordonnance est prête chez le pharmacien.*   My prescription is ready at the pharmacist's.

ordre *m.*   order   *Les noms sont dans l'ordre d'entrée des acteurs en scène.*   The names are in the order of the actors' appearance on the stage.

oreille *f.*   ear   *Il a une bonne oreille pour la musique.*   He has a good ear for music.

oreiller *m.*   pillow   *J'ai besoin d'un autre oreiller, s'il vous plaît.*   I need another pillow, please.

ou   or   *Ils nous donneront la réponse dans cinq ou six jours.*   They will give us the answer in five or six days.

où   where   *Je ne sais pas où il demeure.*   I don't know where he lives.

oublier   to forget   *J'ai oublié d'apporter la carte.*   I forgot to bring the map.

ouest *m.*   west   *A l'ouest de la France est l'océan Atlantique.*   To the west of France is the Atlantic Ocean.

oui   yes   *Oui, je me charge d'acheter les billets.*   Yes, I will take care of buying the tickets.

ouïe *f.*   hearing   *Son ouïe est très mauvaise; il est presque sourd.*   His hearing is very bad; he is almost deaf.

ouvert   open   *Le bureau de tourisme est ouvert de neuf heures à une heure.*   The tourist office is open from nine o'clock to one o'clock.

ouvrir   to open   *Ouvrons la fenêtre pour avoir un peu d'air.*   Let's open the window to have a little air.

page *f.*   page   *Ouvrez vos livres à la page cent.*   Open your books to page one hundred.

paire *f.*   pair   *J'ai besoin d'une paire de ciseaux.*   I need a pair of scissors.

paix *f.*   peace   *J'ai trouvé la paix dans ce petit village.*   I found peace in this little village.

palais *m.*   palace   *Le Palais-Royal de Paris a été construit en 1629 pour Richelieu.*   The Royal Palace in Paris was built in 1629 for Richelieu.

pâle   pale   *Elle a le teint pâle.*   She has a pale complexion.

pantalon *m.*   long pants, trousers   *Aimez-vous le pantalon que je viens d'acheter?*   Do you like the trousers that I have just bought?

papier *m.*   paper   *Il a laissé toutes sortes de papiers sur son bureau.*   He left all kinds of papers on his desk.

paquet *m.*   package   *Il faut apporter ce paquet à la poste.*   This package must be brought to the post office.

par   by   *Ce roman a été écrit par Emile Zola.*   This novel was written by Emile Zola.

paragraphe *m.*   paragraph   *Ecrivez un paragraphe sur le climat en Provence.*   Write a paragraph on the climate in Provence.

paraît que, il   it seems that   *Il paraît qu'elle est malade.*   It seems that she is ill.

paraître   to appear   *Il a paru tout d'un coup devant moi.*   He suddenly appeared in front of me.

parapluie *m.*   umbrella   *Prends ton parapluie parce que le ciel est couvert.*   Take your umbrella because it is cloudy.

parc m. park *Il y a un joli lac dans le parc.* There is a pretty lake in the park.

parce que because *Nous sommes en retard parce que notre voiture a eu une panne.* We are late because our car had a breakdown.

pardon m. pardon (me); forgiveness *Pardon, je suis entré parce que je pensais que la salle était libre.* Pardon me, I came in because I thought the room was free.

parent(e) m./f. relative; parent *Il a beaucoup de parents en France.* He has many relatives in France.

parler to speak, to talk *Il parle bien anglais pour un Français.* He speaks English well for a Frenchman.

parti m. party (political) *Le parti socialiste va gagner, je crois.* The Socialist party will win, I think.

partie f. part *Quelle partie choisissez-vous?* Which part do you choose?

pas m. step, pace *J'entends tes pas et je sais que tu rentres à la maison.* I hear your steps and I know you are returning home.

passage m. aisle *Le passage pour arriver à la sortie est très étroit.* The aisle to reach the exit is very narrow.

passé past, last *Ils sont venus la semaine passée.* They came last week.

passer to pass, to spend *Nous allons passer les vacances en Corse.* We are going to spend the vacation in Corsica.

pastille f. tablet, lozenge *Si vous prenez ces pastilles, vous n'allez pas tousser tellement.* If you take these lozenges, you won't cough so much.

patron m. boss, owner *Le patron insiste sur la ponctualité.* The boss stresses punctuality.

pauvre poor *Cet étudiant est si pauvre qu'il n'a pas assez d'argent pour acheter ses livres.* That student is so poor that he doesn't have enough money to buy his books.

payer to pay *C'est notre tour de payer l'addition.* It's our turn to pay the bill.

payer, faire to charge *Combien faites-vous payer une leçon d'une heure?* How much do you charge for a one-hour lesson?

pays m. country *Les deux pays de France et d'Italie sont divisés par les Alpes.* The two countries of France and Italy are divided by the Alps.

paysage m. landscape *Les paysages de Provence sont très pittoresques.* The landscapes of Provence are very picturesque.

peau f. skin *Elle a la peau délicate.* She has delicate skin.

péché m. sin *Ce n'est pas un péché grave.* It's not a serious sin.

peindre to paint *Cézanne a su peindre la nature d'une nouvelle manière.* Cézanne knew how to paint nature in a new way.

peine *f.*   pain, grief   *Ça me fait de la peine de voir ce petit orphelin.*   It grieves me to see that little orphan.

peinture *f.*   painting   *Le Musée de l'Orangerie a des peintures magnifiques de Monet.*   The Orangerie Museum has some magnificent paintings of Monet.

pellicule *f.*   film   *Je dois faire développer la pellicule qui est dans mon appareil.*   I must have the film that is in my camera developed.

pendant   during   *Pendant notre séjour à Nice, je compte aller nager dans la mer.*   During our stay in Nice, I plan to go swimming in the sea.

pendant que   while   *Pendant qu'elle faisait le marché, j'ai étudié.*   While she was doing the marketing, I studied.

penser   to think, intend   *Que pensez-vous faire? Je pense qu'on devrait partir.*   What do you intend to do? I think that we should leave.

pension *f.*   boardinghouse   *Les pensions sont moins chères que les hôtels et on y mange bien en général.*   Boardinghouses are less expensive than hotels and, in general, you eat well there.

perdre   to lose   *J'ai manqué de perdre mon portefeuille.*   I almost lost my wallet.

permettre   to permit, allow   *Il est allé voir le capitaine mais on ne lui a pas permis de lui parler.*   He went to see the captain but he wasn't allowed to speak to him.

permission *f.*   permission, leave   *Avec votre permission, j'aimerais quitter la réunion pour aller chercher ma fille à l'école.*   With your permission, I would like to leave the meeting to go pick up my daughter at school.

personne   no one, nobody   *Personne n'est arrivé.*   No one arrived.

peser   to weigh   *A l'aéroport on va peser les valises.*   At the airport they will weigh the suitcases.

petit(e)   small, little   *Ma chambre est trop petite.*   My bedroom is too small.

peu, un   a little   *J'aimerais un peu de vin.*   I would like a little wine.

peu de   few, not much, not many   *J'essaie de prendre peu de médicaments, si possible.*   I try to take few medicines, if possible.

peur *f.*   fear   *Il a peur du chien.*   He's afraid of the dog.

peut-être   perhaps, maybe   *Je vais peut-être acheter un ordinateur tout neuf.*   Maybe I will buy a brand-new computer.

photo *f.*   photo   *La photo de mon passeport est très récente.*   The photo on my passport is very recent.

phrase *f.*   sentence, phrase   *Ce paragraphe est bien écrit mais il y a une faute dans la dernière phrase.*   This paragraph is well written but there is a mistake in the last sentence.

pièce *f.*   play; room   *Les pièces de Molière sont intéressantes et amusantes.*   Molière's plays are interesting and amusing.

pied *m.*   foot   *J'ai mal aux pieds parce que j'ai trop marché.*   My feet hurt because I walked too much.

pierre *f.*   stone   *Le puits est construit en pierre.*   The well is built of stone.

piéton *m.*   pedestrian   *Les piétons doivent traverser seulement à feu vert.*   The pedestrians must cross only at the green light.

pilule *f.*   pill   *Le dentiste m'a donné des pilules pour mon mal de dents.*   The dentist gave me some pills for my toothache.

pire   worse, worst   *Le restaurant où nous avons dîné hier était mauvais mais ce restaurant est encore pire.*   The restaurant where we ate yesterday was bad but this restaurant is even worse.

piscine *f.*   swimming pool   *Pour faire de l'exercice, je nage dans la piscine chaque semaine.*   To exercise, I swim in the pool every week.

pittoresque   picturesque   *La Corse a des paysages très pittoresques.*   Corsica has some very picturesque landscapes.

place *f.*   city square; seat, place   *La maison de Victor Hugo est à la place des Vosges à Paris.*   Victor Hugo's house is in Vosges Square in Paris.   *Avez-vous des places libres pour le concert?*   Do you have seats available for the concert?

plafond *m.*   ceiling   *Il faut peindre le plafond de la salle de bains.*   We have to paint the bathroom ceiling.

plage *f.*   beach   *Les plages de la Côte d'Azur sont très belles.*   The beaches of the French Riviera are very beautiful.

plaindre, se   to pity; to complain   *Nous plaignons tous ces immigrés sans-abri.*   We pity all these homeless immigrants.   *De quoi vous plaignez-vous?*   What are you complaining about?

plainte *f.*   complaint   *Ses plaintes ne cessent jamais.*   Her complaints never cease.

plaire   to please, to be likable   *Il nous plaît de voyager en bateau.*   We like to travel by boat.

plaisanterie *f.*   joke   *Nous nous sommes mis à rire quand il a raconté la plaisanterie.*   We started laughing when he told the joke.

plaisir *m.*   pleasure   *C'est un plaisir de vous revoir.*   It's a pleasure to see you again.

plancher *m.*   floor   *Il faut demander un balai pour balayer le plancher.*   We must ask for a broom to sweep the floor.

plat *m.*   dish   *Ce restaurant offre des plats vraiment exquis.*   This restaurant offers some really exquisite dishes.

plein   full   *Cette salle est pleine de soleil.*   This room is full of sun.

pleurer   to cry   *Le poème de Verlaine dit: "Il pleure dans mon coeur, comme il pleut sur la ville."*   Verlaine's poem says: "Tears fall in my heart, as rain falls on the city."

pleuvoir   to rain   *Il va pleuvoir toute la nuit.*   It is going to rain all night.

pluie *f.*   rain   *La pluie arrose les fleurs.*   The rain waters the flowers.

plus   more   *L'essence coûte plus en France qu'aux Etats-Unis.*   Gasoline costs more in France than in the United States.

plusieurs   several   *Plusieurs parents m'ont recommandé cette pension de famille.*   Several relatives have recommended this residential hotel.

poche *f.*   pocket   *Il a mis son portefeuille dans la poche.*   He put his wallet in his pocket.

poésie *f.*   poetry   *La poésie de Baudelaire est magnifique.*   Baudelaire's poetry is magnificent.

poids *m.*   weight   *Le poids de ces pommes est deux kilos.*   The weight of these apples is two kilos.

point *m.*   point, dot   *Il y a deux points en question.*   There are two points in question.   *Il faut mettre un point à la fin de chaque phrase déclarative.*   You must put a period at the end of each declarative sentence.

poitrine *f.*   chest   *Si tu as mal à la poitrine, consulte tout de suite ton médecin.*   If you have pain in your chest, consult your doctor right away.

poli   polite   *Les enfants doivent toujours être polis avec les grandes personnes en France.*   Children must always be polite to older people in France.

police *f.*   police   *La police nous suit.*   The police are following us.

pont *m.*   bridge   *"Le Pont Mirabeau" est un très beau poème de Guillaume Apollinaire.*   "The Mirabeau Bridge" is a very beautiful poem by Guillaume Apollinaire.

port *m.*   port, harbor   *Marseille est un port très important de France.*   Marseille is a very important port of France.

porte *f.*   door   *Fermez la porte à clé quand vous sortez.*   Lock the door when you go out.

portefeuille *m.*   wallet; portfolio   *Je ne trouve pas mon portefeuille.*   I can't find my wallet.

porter   to carry, wear, take   *Il a porté nos valises à notre chambre.*   He carried the suitcases to our room.

porteur *m.*   porter   *Il est difficile de trouver un porteur libre dans cette gare.*   It is difficult to find a porter who is available in this railroad station.

portier *m.*   doorman   *Le portier va nous appeler un taxi.*   The doorman will call a taxi for us.

poste *m.*   position, job   *Je cherche un poste chez le Ministre culturel de France.*   I am looking for a job with the Cultural Minister of France.

poupée *f.*   doll   *J'ai acheté une poupée adorable pour ma petite-fille.*   I have bought an adorable doll for my granddaughter.

pour   for; in order to   *Je pars demain pour la France.*   I am leaving tomorrow for France.

pourboire *m.*   tip   *Il faut laisser un pourboire pour le garçon.*   We must leave a tip for the waiter.

pourquoi?   why?   *Pourquoi n'es-tu pas venu?*   Why didn't you come?

pousser   to push   *J'ai poussé la porte mais elle est restée fermée.*   I pushed the door but it remained closed.

pouvoir   to be able, can   *Pouvez-vous nous aider?*   Can you help us?

premier   first   *Le premier jour du cours il a acheté le texte dont il avait besoin pour faire ses devoirs.*   The first day of the course he bought the textbook which he needed to do his homework.

prendre   to take   *Prenez le métro à la Place de la République.*   Take the metro at Republic Square.

prendre   to (take to) eat, drink   *Que prenez-vous? Je prends une glace au chocolat.*   What are you having? I'm having a chocolate ice cream.

préparer   to prepare   *J'ai préparé le repas pour ce soir.*   I prepared the meal for this evening.

près de   near   *La poste est près de la librairie.*   The post office is near the bookstore.

presque   almost   *Elle arrive presque toujours en retard.*   She almost always arrives late.

pressé   in a hurry   *Elle est pressée parce qu'elle est en retard.*   She is in a hurry because she is late.

prêter   to lend   *Elle m'a prêté sa bicyclette.*   She lent me her bicycle.

preuve *f.*   proof   *Quelles preuves avez-vous qu'il a commis ce crime?*   What proof do you have that he committed this crime?

prison *f.*   jail   *Il est en prison pour un vol.*   He is in jail for theft.

prix *m.*   price, prize   *Les prix dans cette pâtisserie sont très élevés.*   The prices in this pastry shop are very high.

problème *m.*   problem   *Nous devons résoudre ce problème.*   We have to solve this problem.

prochain(e)   next   *La semaine prochaine j'ai rendez-vous chez le dentiste.*   Next week I have an appointment with the dentist.

profit *m.*   profit   *Il a vendu ses actions avec beaucoup de profit.*   He sold his shares with a very good profit.

profiter de   to take advantage of   *Profitez de cette occasion de voir Versailles.*   Take advantage of this opportunity to see Versailles.

projet *m.*   project   *Le patron a approuvé le projet.*   The boss approved the project.

promenade *f.*   walk, ride   *Nous faisons une promenade à travers le parc chaque soir.*   We take a walk across the park every evening.

promesse *f.*   promise   *Elle m'a fait la promesse de rentrer avant minuit.*   She made me a promise to return home before midnight.

propre   clean; [one's] own   *Leurs chambres sont toujours propres.*   Their rooms are always clean.

propriétaire *m./f.*   owner, proprietor   *Le propriétaire désire louer la maison.*   The owner wishes to rent the house.

propriété *f.*   property   *Sa propriété à la campagne est très jolie.*   Her property in the country is very pretty.

protéger   to protect   *Ce chien va nous protéger.*   This dog will protect us.

provisions *f. pl.*   groceries   *On peut acheter toutes sortes de provisions au supermarché.*   You can buy all kinds of groceries at the supermarket.

quai *m.*   platform   *Quel est le quai d'arrivée du train de Lyon?*   On what platform does the train from Lyon arrive?

quand   when   *Quand vas-tu arriver?*   When will you arrive?

quartier *m.*   neighborhood   *Le Quartier Latin est un quartier pour les étudiants à Paris.*   The Latin Quarter is a neighborhood for students in Paris.

que   that; which; who   *Il pense qu'elle partira.*   He thinks that she will leave.

que   what   *Que voulez-vous?*   What do you want?

quelque chose   something   *J'ai vu quelque chose d'intéressant.*   I saw something interesting.

quelques-uns   some, any   *Quelques-uns d'entre vous me connaissent déjà.*   Some of you already know me.

quelqu'un   someone, anyone   *Quelqu'un a téléphoné.*   Someone called.

question *f.*   question   *J'ai une question à vous poser.*   I have a question to ask you.

queue *f.*   line, tail   *Il faut faire une longue queue pour entrer au Musée du Louvre.*   You have to wait on a long line to get into the Louvre Museum.

qui   who, whom   *Le prof avec qui j'ai déjeuné s'appelle Peter.*   The professor with whom I had lunch is named Peter.   *Qui va conduire?*   Who is going to drive?

rabais *m.*   discount, reduction   *Au mois d'août, presque tous les magasins offrent des rabais.*   In August almost all the stores offer discounts.

raison *f.*   reason   *Pascal a dit: Le coeur a ses raisons que la raison ne connaît pas.*   Pascal said: "The heart has its reasons that reason does not know."

raison, avoir   to be right   *Je pense qu'il a raison.*   I think he is right.

rapide   rapid, quick   *Il a fait une décision très rapide.*   He made a very quick decision.

rappeler, se   to remember   *Je me rappelle ce que tu m'as dit.*   I remember what you told me.

raser, se   to shave   *Il a la barbe et donc il n'a pas besoin de se raser.*   He has a beard and therefore he doesn't need to shave.

recevoir   to receive   *Je viens de recevoir un paquet.*   I have just received a package.

reconnaître   to recognize   *J'ai reconnu mon ancien prof de musique à la soirée.*   I recognized my former music professor at the party.

reçu *m.*   receipt   *La douane demandra un reçu.*   Customs will ask for a receipt.

regarder   to look (at)   *Regarde l'aube sur la mer!*   Look at the dawn on the sea!

régime *m.*   regime, diet   *Je dois suivre un régime pour perdre du poids.*   I have to go on a diet to lose weight.

règle *f.*   ruler, rule   *Il faut obéir aux règles de circulation.*   You must obey the traffic rules.

regretter   to regret, to be sorry (for)   *Je le regrette, mais il n'a pas téléphoné.*   I am sorry, but he didn't call.

reine *f.*   queen   *La reine Marie Antoinette a été guillotinée.*   Queen Marie Antoinette was guillotined.

rejeter   to reject   *Ils ont rejeté notre idée.*   They rejected our idea.

remède *m.*   cure, remedy   *Sa maladie est sans remède.*   His illness is without a cure.

remercier   to thank   *Je vous remercie de votre gentillesse.*   I thank you for your kindness.

remettre   hand over, deliver   *Elle m'a remis la lettre sans rien dire.*   She handed me the letter without saying anything.

remplir   to fill   *Remplissez la bouteille d'huile, s'il vous plaît.*   Fill the bottle with oil, please.

rencontrer   to meet, to bump into   *Nous nous sommes rencontrés par hasard au supermarché.*   We met by chance at the supermarket.

rendez-vous *m.*   appointment, date   *J'ai rendez-vous chez le médecin à dix heures.*   I have an appointment at the doctor's office at ten o'clock.

rendre   to return, give back   *Demain je vais te rendre la carte que tu m'as prêtée.*   Tomorrow I am going to return the map that you lent me.

repas *m.*   meal   *On mange de bons repas à cette pension.*   You eat good meals in this boardinghouse.

repasser   to iron, press   *Je dois repasser cette robe avant de la mettre.*   I have to iron this dress before putting it on.

répéter   to repeat   *Je répète,—N'arrivez pas en retard!*   I repeat: Do not arrive late!

répondre   to answer, reply   *Réponds à ma lettre ou je ne t'écrirai plus.*   Answer my letter or I will not write to you anymore.

réponse *f.* answer, reply *Sa réponse était favorable.* His answer was favorable.

reposer, se to rest *Le voyage était long et je désire me reposer.* The trip was long and I want to rest.

respirer to breathe *Il respirait avec difficulté mais il était lucide.* He was breathing with difficulty but he was conscious.

rester to stay, remain *Nous avons l'intention de rester à Paris pour deux semaines.* We plan to stay in Paris for two weeks.

retard *m.* delay *L'avion est parti avec un retard de trois heures.* The plane left after a three-hour delay.

retard, en late *N'arrive pas à la gare en retard.* Don't arrive late at the railroad station.

retarder to be slow, to delay *Ta montre retarde de cinq minutes.* Your watch is five minutes slow.

retirer to withdraw, take out *J'ai retiré de l'argent de la banque pour mon voyage.* I withdrew some money from the bank for my trip.

retour return; **être de __ (de)** to be back (from) *Il sera de retour à six heures.* He'll be back at six o'clock.

retourner to return, go back *J'espère retourner en France.* I hope to return to France.

réunion *f.* meeting; reunion *J'ai manqué la réunion du département parce que j'étais malade.* I missed the departmental meeting because I was sick.

réveiller to awaken, to wake up *Réveillez-moi à 7h demain matin.* Wake me up at 7:00 tomorrow morning.

revenir to come back *Revenez la semaine prochaine et les vêtements seront prêts.* Come back next week and the clothing will be ready.

revue *f.* magazine *On peut acheter la revue* Paris-Match *dans le kiosque au coin de la rue.* You can buy the magazine *Paris-Match* at the stand on the street corner.

rhume *m.* cold (virus) *Avec ce rhume terrible je ne pourrai pas aller à la plage.* With this terrible cold, I will not be able to go to the beach.

riche rich, wealthy *Cet étudiant n'est pas riche; il a gagné une bourse d'études pour étudier à l'étranger.* This student isn't rich; he won a scholarship to study abroad.

rien *m.* nothing *Je n'ai rien à dire.* I have nothing to say.

rire to laugh *Cette comédie m'a vraiment fait rire.* That comedy really made me laugh.

robe *f.* dress *Apportez une robe élégante pour aller au théâtre ou à une soirée.* Bring one elegant dress to go to the theater or to a party.

roi *m.* king *Le roi Louis XVI a été guillotiné.* King Louis XVI was guillotined.

rompre   to break   *Dans un magasin si vous rompez quelque chose vous devez le payer.*   In a store if you break something you must pay for it.

rôti   roasted   *On mange l'agneau rôti pour Pâques.*   Roast lamb is eaten for Easter.

route *f.*   road, way, route   *Il y a beaucoup de marchands de fruits en route.*   There are many fruit vendors on the way.

royal   royal   *Le Palais-Royal est un célebre monument de Paris.*   The Royal Palace is a famous historic building in Paris.

rue *f.*   street   *La rue de notre hôtel est la prochaine.*   The street our hotel is on is the next one.

sable *m.*   sand   *A la plage l'enfant aime jouer avec le sable.*   At the beach the child likes to play with the sand.

sac *m.*   bag, sack   *On examine tous les sacs à l'aéroport.*   All the bags are examined at the airport.

sale   dirty   *Mon verre est sale.*   My glass is dirty.

salle à manger *f.*   dining room   *On dîne dans la salle à manger.*   We eat dinner in the dining room.

salle de bains *f.*   bathroom   *Une chambre avec salle de bains, s'il vous plaît.*   A room with bath, please.

salon *m.*   living room   *Les invités sont dans le salon.*   The guests are in the living room.

saluer   to greet   *J'ai salué mes voisins.*   I greeted my neighbors.

salut   hi, hello   *Salut, comment ça va?*   Hi, how are you?

sang *m.*   blood   *A l'hôpital, il a reçu des transfusions de sang.*   At the hospital he was given some blood transfusions.

sans   without   *Ne sortez pas sans parapluie.*   Don't go out without an umbrella.

santé *f.*   health   *Toute la famille est en bonne santé.*   The whole family is enjoying good health.

satisfait   satisfied   *Il était satisfait de l'entrevue.*   He was satisfied with the interview.

savoir   to know   *Elle ne sait pas si elle va nous rejoindre.*   She doesn't know if she will join us.

savon *m.*   soap   *Il faut acheter du savon pour laver la vaisselle.*   We have to buy soap to wash the dishes.

se   himself, herself, themselves, oneself, one another   *Elles se téléphonent presque tous les jours.*   They call each other almost every day.

sec   dry   *Je prends ces pastilles quand j'ai la gorge sèche.*   I take these cough drops when I have a dry throat.

sécher   to dry   *Je dois faire sécher le linge.*   I have to get the laundry dried.

second *m.* second *Dans trois seconds minuit sonnera.* In three seconds midnight will strike.

selon according to *Selon mon comptable, ce n'est pas le bon moment d'investir son argent dans la bourse.* According to my accountant this is not a good time to invest in the stock market.

semaine *f.* week *Nous comptons passer deux semaines dans les Alpes.* We are counting on spending two weeks in the Alps.

sentir to feel; to smell *Tout sent bon dans la cuisine!* Everything smells good in the kitchen!

sentir, se to feel *Je ne vais pas au pique-nique, parce que je ne me sens pas bien.* I am not going to the picnic, because I don't feel well.

séparer to separate *La Manche sépare la France de l'Angleterre.* The English Channel separates France from England.

sérieux (euse) serious *C'est une maladie sérieuse.* It's a serious illness.

serveur (euse) waiter, waitress *On appelle celui qui sert à table un garçon ou un serveur.* The one who serves at the table is called a waiter.

service *m.* service *Le service est excellent dans cet hôtel.* The service is excellent in this hotel.

serviette *f.* napkin; towel; briefcase *Garçon, j'ai besoin d'une serviette.* Waiter, I need a napkin.

servir to serve *On sert le petit déjeuner à huit heures.* Breakfast is served at eight o'clock.

seul alone, only *Je suis seule à la maison depuis quatre jours.* I have been home alone for four days. *Elle seule sait m'aider.* Only she knows how to help me.

seulement only *Je suis allé à l'université seulement pour revoir mon ancien prof de français.* I went to the university only to see my former French teacher again.

si if, whether *S'il pleut on ira au musée d'art.* If it rains we will go to the art museum.

siècle *m.* century *En France, le dix-septième siècle est l'époque de la littérature classique.* In France, the seventeenth century is the period of classical literature.

signal *m.* signal *Quand tu entends deux coups de fil, ce sera le signal que je pars.* When you hear two rings on the phone, that will be the signal that I'm leaving.

signature *f.* signature *La banque a besoin de votre signature.* The bank needs your signature.

signer to sign *J'ai signé le chèque.* I signed the check.

simple simple, easy *La carte de métro est simple à suivre.* The Metro map is easy to follow.

soie *f.*   silk   *Mon amie m'a donné un foulard de soie.*   My friend gave me a silk scarf.

soif *f.*   thirst   *Il faut boire quand on a soif.*   You must drink when you're thirsty.

soigner, se   to take care of (oneself)   *Soigne-toi. Ne tombe pas malade.*   Take care of yourself. Don't get sick.

soir *m.*   evening, night   *Hier soir nous sommes allés au théâtre.*   Last night we went to the theater.

soleil *m.*   sun   *Le soleil est sur le point de se coucher.*   The sun is about to set.

sommeil *m.*   sleep   *Je vais m'endormir tout de suite parce que j'ai très sommeil.*   I am going to go to sleep right away because I'm very sleepy.

son   his, her   *Elle m'a présenté à son père.*   She introduced me to her father.

soudain   suddenly   *Soudain il a commencé à pleuvoir.*   Suddenly it began to rain.

souhait *m.*   wish, greeting   *Meilleurs souhaits à tes parents.*   Best wishes to your parents.

soulier *m.*   shoe   *Mes souliers neufs sont confortables.*   My new shoes are comfortable.

souper   to eat supper   *On soupe vers huit heures et demie en France.*   People have supper around eight-thirty in France.

souper *m.*   supper   *Le souper est un repas simple.*   Supper is a simple meal.

sourire   to smile   *T'es-tu rappelé de sourire quand on a fait ta photo?*   Did you remember to smile when they took your picture?

sous   under   *Ils l'ont laissé sous la table.*   They left it under the table.

souvenir, se (de)   to remember   *Vous souvenez-vous de mon frère Henri?*   Do you remember my brother Henry?

souvent   often   *Il me téléphone souvent.*   He calls me often.

spectacle *m.*   performance, show   *Pour les enfants, le Cirque du Soleil est un spectacle inoubliable.*   For children, "le Cirque du Soleil" is an unforgettable show.

sport *m.*   sport   *Le sport favori des Français est le football.*   The favorite sport of the French is soccer.

statue *f.*   statue   *La France a donné aux Etats-Unis la statue de "la Liberté éclairant le monde."*   France gave the United States the statue of "Liberty Enlightening the World."

stylo *m.*   pen   *Apportez un stylo à votre examen, s'il vous plaît.*   Bring a pen to your exam, please.

subvenir aux besoins de   to support (financially)   *Il subvient aux besoins de six personnes.*   He supports six people.

succès *m.* success *Son dernier film a eu beaucoup de succès.* His last movie was very successful.

sud *m.* south *Nice est au sud.* Nice is to the south.

suffire to suffice, to be enough *Cela suffit. Je n'en veux plus.* That's enough. I don't want any more.

suivant following, next *Le premier jour à Paris nous avons vu nos amis et le jour suivant on est allé au Louvre.* The first day in Paris we saw our friends and the following day we went to the Louvre.

suivre to follow *Suivez-moi et je vous montrerai la rue que vous cherchez.* Follow me and I will show you the street that you are looking for.

sujet de, au about *Avez-vous un livre au sujet de la deuxième guerre mondiale?* Do you have a book on the Second World War?

supporter to stand, tolerate *Je ne supporte pas tout ce bruit dans la rue.* I can't stand all that noise in the street.

sur on, on top of *Il y a un moulin à vent sur la colline.* There is a windmill on the hill.

sûr sure, certain *J'étais sûr de recevoir un bon accueil.* I was sure of receiving a good welcome.

sympathique nice, friendly, pleasant *La plupart de mes compagnons de voyage étaient sympathiques.* Most of my traveling companions were nice.

tabac *m.* tobacco *On achète les timbres chez le marchand de tabac.* You buy stamps at the tobacco shop.

table *f.* table *Nous avons une petite table dans la cuisine.* We have a small table in the kitchen.

tableau(x) *m.* picture, painting *Le Louvre a de très beaux tableaux de David et d'Ingres parmi quelques-uns des meilleurs tableaux du monde.* The Louvre has some very beautiful paintings by David and by Ingres among others of the best paintings in the world.

taille *f.* size *Quelle taille portez-vous?* Which size do you wear?

tasse *f.* cup *Je désire une tasse de café, s'il vous plaît.* I want a cup of coffee, please.

taureau *m.* bull *A Arles j'ai vu une course de taureaux.* In Arles I saw a bullfight.

tee-shirt *m.* T-shirt, undershirt *Les jeunes gens portent souvent des tee-shirts au lieu des chemises.* Young men often wear T-shirts instead of shirts.

tel, telle such *Je n'ai jamais entendu dire une telle chose!* I have never heard such a thing!

téléphone *m.* telephone *Je vais me servir du téléphone dans la cabine téléphonique au coin de la rue.* I am going to use the telephone in the phone booth at the street corner.

tempête *f.*   storm   *Après cette tempête il fera plus frais.*   After this storm it will be cooler.

temps *m.*   time, weather   *Je n'ai pas le temps d'aller au cinéma.* I don't have time to go to the movies.   *Il a fait mauvais temps ce week-end.* The weather was bad this weekend.

tenir   to hold, to keep   *Il tient toujours ses promesses.*   He always keeps his promises.

terre *f.*   land, earth   *La terre de cette ferme est tres fertile.*   This farm's land is very fertile.

tête *f.*   head   *J'ai mal à la tête ce matin.*   I have a headache this morning.

théâtre *m.*   theater   *La Comédie Française est le théâtre où l'on présente les pièces de Molière.*   The Comédie Française is the theater that shows Molière's plays.

timbre *m.*   stamp   *Je vais à la poste pour acheter des timbres.*   I am going to the post office to buy stamps.

toilette *f.*   rest room; toilet   *Les toilettes sont en bas.*   The rest rooms are downstairs.

tomber   to fall   *Elle est tombée sur les genoux en traversant la rue.*   She fell on her knees while crossing the street.

ton   your *(s. fam.)*   *Ton passeport est-il prêt?*   Is your passport ready?

tôt   early   *Il est arrivé très tôt ce matin.*   He arrived very early this morning.

toucher   to touch   *Regardez mais ne touchez pas, dit le marchand de fruits.*   Look but don't touch, says the fruit vendor.

toujours   always   *Elle arrive toujours à l'heure.*   She always arrives on time.

tour *f.*   tower   *La Tour de Londres était une fois une prison d'état.*   The Tower of London was once a state prison.

tourner   to turn   *Tournez le coin et vous verrez le stade.*   Turn the corner and you will see the stadium.

tous *m. pl.*   all, everybody   *Nous sommes tous arrivés.*   We all have arrived.

tous les deux   both   *Je les aime tous les deux.*   I like them both.

tout   all, everything   *C'est tout ce que je sais.*   That's all I know.

toux *f.*   cough   *Ta toux m'inquiète.*   Your cough worries me.

traduire   to translate   *Peux-tu traduire ce manuscrit de français en anglais?*   Can you translate this manuscript from French to English?

train *m.*   train   *Prenez un TGV (train à grande vitesse) pour faire un long voyage.*   Take a high-speed train for a long trip.

travail *m.*   work   *Je n'ai pas fini mon travail.*   I haven't finished my work.

travailler to work *Il travaille chez la Banque de France depuis dix ans.* He has been working for the Banque de France for ten years.

traverser to cross *Fais attention quand tu traverses la rue.* Be careful when you cross the street.

très very *Mes enfants vont très bien, merci.* My children are very well, thank you.

triste sad *J'ai dû le rendre triste quand je lui ai dit que son prof de français était mort.* I must have made him sad when I told him that his French professor had died.

tromper to deceive *Il m'a trompé. Il n'a pas rendu l'argent.* He deceived me. He did not return the money.

tromper, se to be mistaken, to be wrong *Il s'est trompé; ce chemin ne mène pas au château.* He was mistaken; this road does not lead to the castle.

trop too; too much *Ceci coûte trop.* This costs too much.

trouver, se to find, (to be located) *Où se trouvent les Jardins de Versailles?* Where are the Versailles gardens located?

tu you (s. fam.) *Tu es le premier à arriver.* You are the first to arrive.

typique typical *La salade niçoise est une nourriture typique de la région près de Nice.* Niçoise salad is a typical food of the area near Nice.

un *m.*, **une** *f.* a, an *J'ai un couteau et une fourchette.* I have a knife and a fork.

usine *f.* factory *Cette usine est pour la fabrication des ordinateurs.* That factory is for the manufacture of computers.

utile useful *Il est utile d'étudier les langues étrangères.* It's useful to study foreign languages.

utiliser to use *On utilise cet insecticide depuis deux ans.* We have been using this insecticide for two years.

vacances *f. pl.* vacation *J'ai déjà commencé mes vacances.* I have already started my vacation.

valise *f.* suitcase *J'essaie de voyager avec une seule valise.* I try to travel with only one suitcase.

vallée *f.* valley *Il fait plus chaud ici dans la vallée que dans les montagnes.* It's hotter here in the valley than in the mountains.

valoir to be worth *Ce terrain ne vaut rien.* This piece of land is worth nothing.

vélo *m.* bike *Les jeunes gens aiment faire des excursions à vélo.* Young people like to go on bike trips.

vendeur (euse) salesclerk *La vendeuse viendra vous aider tout de suite.* The salesclerk will come to help you right away.

vendre   to sell   *Les caricatures qu'on vend à Montmartre sont de bonne qualité.*   The caricatures that are sold in Montmartre are of good quality.

venir   to come   *Peux-tu venir avec nous?*   Can you come with us?

vent *m.*   wind   *Il y a toujours du vent près de la mer.*   It is always windy near the sea.

vérifier   to ascertain, find out   *Je vais vérifier si ses instructions sont justes.*   I am going to find out if his instructions are accurate.

véritable   true, real   *C'est un véritable plaisir de faire la connaissance de ta famille.*   It's a real pleasure to meet your family.

vérité *f.*   truth   *Croyez-vous qu'il ait dit la vérité?*   Do you believe he told the truth?

verre *m.*   glass   *Un verre d'eau minérale va m'enlever la soif.*   A glass of mineral water is going to quench my thirst.

vers   toward   *Il marchait vers la ville où il serait mis en prison.*   He was walking toward the town where he would be put in prison.

veste *f.*   jacket   *J'enlève ma veste parce qu'il fait chaud.*   I'm taking off my jacket because it's warm.

vide   empty   *Les rues sont vides parce qu'une tempête s'approche du quartier.*   The streets are empty because a storm is approaching the neighborhood.

vie *f.*   life   *La vie est pleine de surprises.*   Life is full of surprises.

vieux/vieille   (n.) old man/old woman; **vieux/vieil, vieille** (adj.) old   *Le vieux devant nous a quatre-vingt-douze ans.*   The old man in front of us is ninety-two years old.   *C'est une vieille habitude de donner les muguets en cadeau le premier mai.*   It's an old custom to give a gift of lilies of the valley on the first of May.

village *m.*   village   *Les villages dans les Alpes sont très pittoresques.*   The villages in the Alps are very picturesque.

ville *f.*   city   *Paris est une ville très ancienne et très belle.*   Paris is a very ancient and beautiful city.

vitesse *f.*   speed   *Il est parti à toute vitesse sans dire où il allait.*   He took off at full speed without saying where he was going.

vivre   to live   *Il faut vivre pleinement chaque jour.*   One must live each day fully.

voir   to see   *Que voyez-vous de votre fenêtre?*   What do you see from your window?

voisin *m.*   neighbor   *Mes voisins sont presque tous sympathiques.*   Almost all of my neighbors are nice.

voiture *f.*   car, automobile   *Nous allons voyager en voiture.*   We are going to travel by car.

voix *f.*   voice   *Parlez à haute voix quand vous faites votre discours.*   Speak in a loud voice when you give your speech.

vol *m.* flight; theft *Il va arriver avec un vol de nuit.* He will arrive with a night flight.

voler to fly; to steal *Si vous volez avec Air France vous allez manger bien.* If you fly Air France you will eat well.

voleur *m.* thief *Le voleur s'est échappé avec mon vélo.* The thief escaped with my bike.

voter to vote *Il faut bien voter aux élections.* You must certainly vote in the elections.

vouloir dire to mean *Que veut dire ce billet?* What does this note mean?

vous you *(s. pol.; pl.)* *Comment allez-vous?* How are you?

voyage *m.* trip *Pendant ce voyage j'ai connu plusieurs individus intéressants et très aimables.* During this trip I met several interesting and very kind individuals.

voyager to travel *On devient plus sage si l'on voyage.* You become wiser if you travel.

voyageur/euse *m./f.* traveler *Les voyageurs attendent de savoir la cause du retard.* The travelers are waiting to know the cause of the delay.

vraiment really *Je n'ai vraiment aucune idée.* I really have no idea.

vue *f.* sight, view *De la terrasse il y avait la vue magnifique du Mont Blanc.* From the terrace there was the magnificent view of Mont Blanc.

wagon-lit *m.* sleeper, sleeping car *Pour aller en train, de Bourg St. Maurice dans les Alpes françaises en Italie, j'ai pris une couchette en wagon-lit.* In order to go by train from Bourg St. Maurice in the French Alps to Italy, I took a berth in a sleeping car.

La famille   The family

beau-frère (belle-soeur)   brother-in-law, sister-in-law
beau-père (belle-mère)   father-in-law, mother-in-law
belle-fille, bru (gendre, beau-fils)   daughter-in-law, son-in-law
cousin (-e)   cousin
femme   wife
fille (fils)   daughter, son
frère   brother
grand-mère (grand-père)   grandmother, grandfather

mari   husband
mère   mother
neveu   nephew
nièce   niece
oncle   uncle
père   father
petit-fils (petite-fille)   grandson, granddaughter
soeur   sister
tante   aunt

Les jours de la semaine   The days of the week

lundi *m.*   Monday
mardi *m.*   Tuesday
mercredi *m.*   Wednesday
jeudi *m.*   Thursday

vendredi *m.*   Friday
samedi *m.*   Saturday
dimanche *m.*   Sunday

Les mois de l'année   The months of the year

janvier January
février February
mars March
avril April
mai May
juin June

juillet July
août August
septembre September
octobre October
novembre November
décembre December

Les saisons   The seasons

le printemps *m.*   spring
l'été *m.*   summer

l'automne *m.*   autumn
l'hiver *m.*   winter

Les nombres   Numbers

zéro   0
un   1
deux   2
trois   3
quatre   4

cinq   5
six   6
sept   7
huit   8
neuf   9

dix   10
onze   11
douze   12
treize   13
quatorze   14
quinze   15
seize   16
dix-sept   17
dix-huit   18
dix-neuf   19
vingt   20
vingt et un   21
vingt-deux   22
trente   30
trente et un   31
trente-deux   32
quarante   40
cinquante   50
soixante   60

soixante-dix   70
quatre-vingts   80
quatre-vingt-dix   90
cent   100
cent et un   101
cent-deux   102
deux cents   200
trois cents   300
quatre cents   400
cinq cents   500
six cents   600
sept cents   700
huit cents   800
neuf cents   900
mille   1,000
deux mille   2,000
cent mille   100,000
un million   1,000,000
deux millions   2,000,000

Les couleurs   Colors

la couleur *f.*   the color
le blanc *m.*   white
le bleu *m.*   blue
le brun *m.*   brown
le gris *m.*   gray
le jaune *m.*   yellow
le marron *m.*   chestnut

le noir *m.*   black
l'orange *m.*   orange
le pourpre *m.*   purple
le rose *m.*   pink
le rouge *m.*   red
le vert *m.*   green

La nourriture   Food

abricot *m.*   apricot
agneau *m.*   lamb
ail *m.*   garlic
amande *f.*   almond
ananas *m.*   pineapple
anchois *m.*   anchovy
artichaut *m.*   artichoke
asperge *f.*   asparagus
aubergine *f.*   eggplant
avocat *m.*   avocado
baguette *f.*   long, thin French
  bread
beignet *m.*   fritter
beurre *m.*   butter
bière *f.*   beer
bifteck *m.*   steak
biscuit *m.*   biscuit, cookie

boeuf *m.*   beef
bouillabaisse *f.*   fish soup
bouillon *m.*   broth
café *m.*   coffee
calmar *m.*   squid
canard *m.*   duck
carotte *f.*   carrot
cassis *m.*   black-currant (wine)
céleri *m.*   celery
cerise *f.*   cherry
champagne *m.*   champagne
champignon *m.*   mushroom
châtaigne *f.*   chestnut
chou *m.*   cabbage
chou-fleur *m.*   cauliflower
citrouille *f.*   pumpkin
concombre *m.*   cucumber

confiture f. marmalade

coquillages, crustacés m. pl. shellfish

cornichon m. pickle, gherkin

côtelette f. cutlet, chop

crabe m. crab

crème f. cream

crème caramel m. caramel custard

crème fouettée f. whipped cream

crevettes f. pl. shrimp

croissant m. crescent roll

croque-monsieur m. toasted ham-and-cheese sandwich

dessert m. dessert

digestif m. after-dinner liqueur

dinde f. turkey

eau f. water

épinards m. pl. spinach

figue f. fig

filet m. tenderloin, loin

foie m. liver

fraise f. strawberry

framboise f. raspberry

fromage m. cheese

fruit m. fruit

gâteau m. cake

glace f. ice cream

hamburger m. hamburger

haricots m. pl. beans

haricots verts m. pl. green beans

homard m. lobster

huile f. oil

huître f. oyster

jambon m. ham

jus m. juice

lait m. milk

laitue f. lettuce

lapin m. rabbit

lard m. fat, bacon

légume m. vegetable

lentille f. lentil

limonade f. lemonade

maïs m. corn

melon m. melon

merlu m. hake

miel m. honey

morue f. cod

moutarde f. mustard

mouton m. mutton

navet m. turnip

noix f. nut, walnut

noix de coco f. coconut

nouilles f. pl. noodles, pasta

oignon m. onion

olive f. olive

omelette f. omelet

orange f. orange

pain m. bread

pain grillé m. toast

palourde f. clam

pamplemousse m. grapefruit

pastèque f. watermelon

pâtes f. pl. macaroni, pasta

pâtisserie f. pastry

pêche f. peach

petit pain m. roll

poire f. pear

poireau m. leek

pois, petits m. pl. peas

pomme f. apple

pomme de terre f. potato

poisson m. fish

poivre m. pepper

porc m. pork

potage m. soup

poulet m. chicken

prune f. plum

radis m. radish

rafraîchissement m. cool drink

raisin m. grape(s)

raisin sec m. raisin(s)

riz m. rice

salade f. salad

sandwich m. sandwich

sauce f. sauce

saucisse f. sausage, hot dog

saucisson m. slicing sausage

sel m. salt

sorbet m. sherbet

sucre m. sugar

tarte f. pie

thé m. tea

thon m. tuna

tomate f. tomato

truite *f.*   trout
veau *m.*   veal
viande *f.*   meat

vin *m.*   wine
vinaigre *m.*   vinegar
yaourt *m.*   yogurt

Les magasins — Stores

bijouterie *f.*   jewelry store
blanchisserie *f.*   laundry
boucherie *f.*   butcher shop
boulangerie *f.*   bakery (bread)
charcuterie *f.*   delicatessen, pork store
chaussures, magasin de *m.*   shoe store
coiffeur *m.*, chez le   at the barber's, hairdresser's
grand magasin *m.*   department store

librairie *f.*   bookstore
mercerie *f.*   haberdashery
pâtisserie *f.*   cake and pastry shop
pharmacie *f.*   pharmacy
pharmacie-droguerie *f.*   drugstore
quincaillerie *f.*   hardware store
supermarché *m.*   supermarket
teinturerie *f.*   dry cleaner's

Les occupations — Occupations

architecte *m./f.*   architect
artiste *m./f.*   artist
avocat (e)   lawyer
banquier (ière)   banker
boulanger (ère)   baker (bread)
coiffeur (euse)   hairdresser
dentiste *m./f.*   dentist
docteur *m./f.*   doctor (Ph.D., etc.)
infirmier (ière)   nurse

ingénieur *m./f.*   engineer
médecin *m./f.*   doctor (physician)
menuisier *m.*   carpenter
pâtissier(ière)   confectioner, pastry baker
professeur *m./f.*   teacher, professor
secrétaire *m./f.*   secretary
tailleur *m.*   tailor
vendeur (euse)   salesperson

Les animaux — Animals

aigle *m.*   eagle
chat *m.*   cat
cheval *m.*   horse
chèvre *f.*   goat
chien *m.*   dog
grenouille *f.*   frog
lion *m.*   lion
loup *m.*   wolf
mouton *m.*   sheep

oiseau *m.*   bird
ours *m.*   bear
pigeon *m.*   pigeon
renard *m.*   fox
singe *m.*   monkey
souris *f.*   mouse
tigre *m.*   tiger
vache *f.*   cow
zèbre *m.*   zebra

VOCABULARY TIPS

Many words in English and French are the same in spelling and meaning. Others have just slight differences in spelling and can be identified easily. Study the vocabulary hints below.

1. Examples of words that are spelled the same way in both languages:

monument   six   prudent   variable   probable
radio   situation client   principal tropical

2. Many -*er* verbs add a final -*r* to the English verb:

amuse*r*   compare*r*   encourage*r* guide*r*   place*r*
admire*r*   continue*r* dine*r*   oblige*r* tremble*r*

3. The English ending -*y* usually corresponds to the French -*é*, -*ie*, or -*i*:

anxiét*é*   beaut*é*   curiosit*é*   responsabilit*é*
mélancol*ie* cérémon*ie* pharmac*ie*   photograph*ie*
essa*i*   emplo*i*   déla*i*   convo*i*

4. English -*al* often corresponds to French -*el* (f. -elle):

étern*el*   intellectu*el*   matern*el*   offici*el*

5. Often, English -*oun* corresponds to French -*on*:

prof*on*d   f*on*taine   pron*on*cer

6. English -*ous* is sometimes French -*eux* (f. -euse):

curi*eux*   danger*eux*   génér*eux*   joy*eux*

54